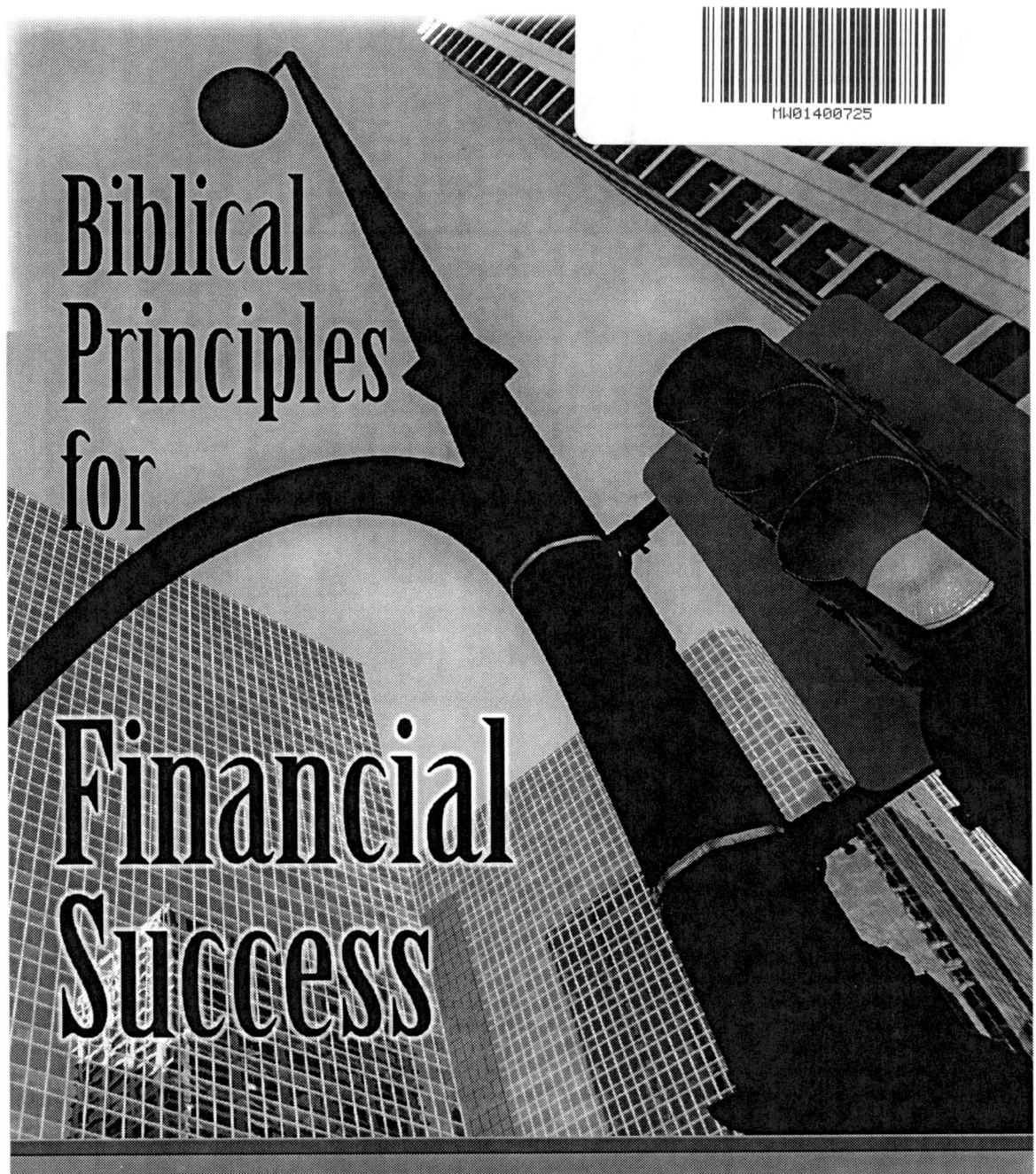

Published by
ABC Book Publishing

AbcBookPublishing.com
Printed in U.S.A.

Biblical Principles for Financial Success
Teacher Workbook

© Copyright 2008 by Richard A. Brott
10 Digit ISBN: 1-60185-015-8
13 Digit ISBN (EAN): 978-1-60185-015-7

All scripture quotations, unless otherwise indicated, are taken from the *Holy Bible, New International Version*®. *NIV*®. Copyright © 1973, 1978, 1984 by International Bible Society. Used by permission of Zondervan Publishing House. All rights reserved.

Other Versions used are:
AMP- Amplified Bible.
Amer. Std.-American Standard Version, 1901.
KJV-King James Version. Authorized King James Version.
NASB-Scripture taken from the *New American Standard Bible*, ©1960, 1962, 1963, 1968, 1971, 1972, 1973, 1975, 1977 by The Lockman Foundation. Used by permission.
Scripture taken from the *New King James Version*. Copyright © 1979, 1980, 1982 by Thomas Nelson, Inc. Publishers. Used by permission. All rights reserved.
Verses marked (*TLB*) are taken from *The Living Bible* © 1971. Used by permission of Tyndale House Publishers, Inc., Wheaton, IL 60189. All rights reserved.
Scripture taken from *THE MESSAGE: The Bible in Contemporary Language* © 2002 by Eugene H. Peterson. All rights reserved.

All rights reserved, including the right to reproduce this book, or any portions thereof, in any form. No part of this book may be reproduced or transmitted in any form or by any means, electronic or mechanical, magnetic, chemical, optical, manual, or otherwise, including photocopying, recording, or by any information storage or retrieval system without written permission from Richard A. Brott. All rights for publishing this book or portions thereof in other languages are contracted by the author.

This publication is designed to provide interesting reading material and general information with regard to the subject matter covered. It is printed, distributed and sold with the understanding that neither the publisher nor the author is engaged in rendering religious, family, legal, accounting, business, investing, financial, credit, debt or other professional advice. If any such advice is required, the services of a competent professional person should be sought. In summary, the content contained herein is not given as advice, rather it is strictly for the purpose of your reading entertainment.

Every effort has been made to supply complete and accurate information. However, neither the publisher nor the author assumes any responsibility for its use, nor for any infringements of patents or other rights of third parties that would result.

First Edition, January, 2008
Richard A. Brott
All Rights Reserved

About the Author

Rich Brott holds a Bachelor of Science degree in Busiess and Economics and a Master of Business Administration.

Rich has served in an executive position with som very successful businesses. He has functioned on the board of directors for churches, businesses, and charities and served on a college advisory board.

He has authored over twenty books:
- *5 Simple Keys to Financial Freedom*
- *10 Life-Changing Attitudes That Will Make You a Finacial Success*
- *15 Biblical Responsibilities Leading to Financial Wisdo1*
- *30 Biblical Principles for Managing Your Money*
- *35 Keys to Financial Independence*
- *A Biblical Perspective On Tithing & Giving*
- *Basic Principles for Maximizing Your Personal Cash Flw*
- *Basic Principles of Conservative Investing*
- *Biblical Principles for Becoming Debt Free*
- *Biblical Principles for Building a Successful Business*
- *Biblical Principles For Financial Success - Student Wrkbook*
- *Biblical Principles For Financial Success - Teacher Workbook*
- *Biblical Principles for Overcoming Discouragement*
- *Biblical Principles for Personal Evangelism (out of print)*
- *Biblical Principles for Releasing Financial Provision*
- *Biblical Principles for Staying Out of Debt*
- *Biblical Principles for Success in Personal Finance*
- *Biblical Principles That Create Success Through Productivity*
- *Business, Occupations, Profession & Vocations in the Bible*
- *Family Finance Student Workbook*
- *Family Finance Teacher Workbook*
- *Public Relations for the Local Church (out of print)*

Rich and his wife Karen have been married for 35 years. He resides in Portland, Oregon, with his wife, three children, son-in-law and granddaughter.

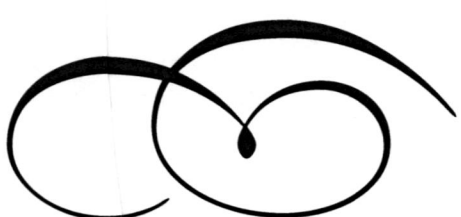

Contents

Introduction 7

Module 1 - God's Economy
Lesson One: Money in God's Economy 13
Lesson Two: The Cycle of Money 25
Lesson Three: The Blessing of Giving 35

Module 2 - Man's Stewardship
Lesson Four: Principles of a Blessed Person 49
Lesson Five: Persona of a Steward 59
Lesson Six: Disciplines of a Steward 69

Module 3 - Family Decisions
Lesson Seven: How to Make Wise Family Decisions 81
Lesson Eight: Facing Financial Challenges 89
Lesson Nine: Defining Your Financial Future 95

Module 4 - Spending Management
Lesson Ten: Managing Your Cash Flow..107
Lesson Eleven: Financial Benefits of Budgeting....................................113
Lesson Twelve: Designing the Perfect Budget......................................121
Lesson Thirteen: Developing the Savings Habit 129
Lesson Fourteen: Borrowing and Credit Issues 137

Module 5 - Making Lifestyle Changes
Lesson Fifteen: Getting out of Debt...147
Lesson Sixteen: Making Lifestyle Changes 157
Lesson Seventeen: Areas of Financial Vulnerability 167

Module 6 - Investing with a Vision
Lesson Eighteen: Investing for your Future 175
Lesson Nineteen: Planning for Retirement 185
Lesson Twenty: Preparing for the Unexpected 193

Answer Key 196

Introduction

1. **This Course Is About Lifestyle**
    a. Living According to Certain Biblical Principles
    b. Enjoying God's Blessing
    c. Living in Peace with Yourself and Your Family

2. **Understanding the Bigger Picture**
    a. Your Attitude Toward Life
    b. Your Understanding of God's Purpose
    c. Your Lifestyle of Christian Stewardship

3. **Stewardship**
    a. It involves every area of our being.
    b. Exercising good personal discipline every day will help me even in difficult circumstances.
    c. Practical resource and financial management are second to Biblical principles.
    d. Stewardship is allowing the Lord to direct our lives; this produces the Biblical "abundant and prosperous life."

4. **Problems**
    a. Problems, financial and otherwise, are common to all people.
    b. Problems should be faced with a calm and confident attitude, knowing that God's resources are available, and that He cares for us.

    "And even the very hairs of your head are all numbered." (Matthew 10:30)

5. **Temptation to Indulge in Short-Term Pleasure**
    a. Self-discipline is necessary when faced with temptation that will cause you to stray from financial goals and personal vision.
    b. Temptation is not the cause of trouble or wrong-doing, but our choices determine right or wrong action.
    c. Set goals and establish definite steps to reach them.

Biblical Principles for Financial Success Teacher Workbook

6. **Family Dynamics**
   a. Clear communication between spouses concerning finance is necessary.
   b. Parents must be an example of wise financial stewards.
   c. Be flexible and admit when mistakes have happened.

7. **Money**
   a. What we are is more important than what we possess.
   b. Our handling of money should reflect God's interest in what He has entrusted to us.

8. **Principles Addressed in This Course**
   a. Time that is planned and invested wisely will bring future benefit.
   b. Honesty, integrity and accountability are more important than wealth.
   c. Getting out of debt and investing for the future require attitude before action.
   d. Spending management is necessary for future success.
   e. We live in this world, but we seek a heavenly reward.

   "Do not store up for yourselves treasures on earth, where moth and rust destroy, and where thieves break in and steal. But store up for yourselves treasures in heaven, where moth and rust do not destroy, and where thieves do not break in and steal. For where your treasure is, there your heart will be also." (Matthew 6:19-21)

Module 1

God's Economy

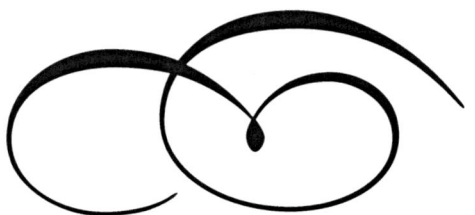

Lesson One

MONEY IN GOD'S ECONOMY

In his heart, a man plans his course, but the LORD determines his steps.
PROVERBS 16:9

Make all you can, save all you can, give all you can.
JOHN WESLEY

Money never made a man happy yet, nor will it. There is nothing in its nature to
produce happiness. The more a man has, the more he wants.
Instead of filling a vacuum, it makes one.
BENJAMIN FRANKLIN

Lesson One

MONEY IN GOD'S ECONOMY

1. **Introduction**
   a. Ordering your life according to God's values and _principles_ will make you successful.
   b. A value system built on dishonesty, lying, cheating and stealing leads to disaster.

2. **Success in God's Economy**
   Those who live according to God's principles can _anticipate_ the wealth and treasure awaiting them in heaven, which outweighs the temporal wealth of this world.

3. **Material Possessions**
   a. Contentment must be a _guiding_ value.
   b. When we have abundance, our lives are not to be caught up in our possessions.

   "Then he said to them, 'Watch out! Be on your guard against all kinds of greed; a man's life does not consist in the abundance of his possessions.'" (Luke 12:15)

   c. The Lord is our _provider_ and substance.

   "But godliness with contentment is great gain. For we brought nothing into the world, and we can take nothing out of it. But if we have food and clothing, we will be content with that. People who want to get rich fall into temptation and a trap and into many foolish and harmful desires that plunge men into ruin and destruction.

For the love of money is a root of all kinds of evil. Some people, eager for money, have wandered from the faith and pierced themselves with many griefs. But you, man of God, flee from all this, and pursue righteousness, godliness, faith, love, endurance and gentleness." (I Timothy 6:6-11)

4. **Real Contentment**
   a. Money cannot buy _contentment_ or happiness.
   b. People find happiness in proportion to the degree that they give.
   c. Those who are "in Christ" have the _opportunity_ to be content.
   d. Recognize your treasures: the love of family and friends, etc.

If our possessions belong to God, nothing is powerful enough to take them away.

---

5. **The Love of Money**

   "Once when we were going to the place of prayer, we were met by a slave girl who had a spirit by which she predicted the future. She earned a great deal of money for her owners by fortune-telling...

   She kept this up for many days. Finally Paul became so troubled that he turned around and said to the spirit, 'In the name of Jesus Christ I command you to come out of her!' At that moment the spirit left her.

   When the owners of the slave girl realized that their hope of making money was gone, they seized Paul and Silas and dragged them into the marketplace to face the authorities...

   The crowd joined in the attack against Paul and Silas, and the magistrates ordered them to be stripped and beaten. After they had been severely flogged, they were thrown into prison, and the jailer was commanded to guard them carefully. Upon

Lesson 1: Money in God's Economy

receiving such orders, he put them in the inner cell and fastened their feet in the stocks." (Acts 16:16, 18, 19, 22-24)

   a. The love of money causes __harm__ to others.
   b. The love of money values possessions over people.
   c. The love of money gets rich off of __human__ weakness.

6. **What I Am, Not What I Possess**
   a. God places importance on the methods used to make money.

   "Fools mock at making amends for sin, but goodwill is found among the upright." (Proverbs 14:9)

   "The house of the righteous contains great treasure, but the income of the wicked brings them trouble." (Proverbs 15:6)

   b. Shedding all sense of __morals__ for the sake of money is foolish.
   c. God rewards faithfulness and enables greater ministry through generosity.

   "... 'Well done, good and faithful servant! You have been faithful with a few things; I will put you in charge of many things. Come and share your master's happiness.'" (Matthew 25:21)

   "You will be enriched in everything for all liberality." (II Corinthians 9:11)

7. **Lack of Contentment**
   a. Don't allow what you don't have to __rob__ you of the joy of gratefulness.

   "You shall not covet your neighbor's house. You shall not covet your neighbor's wife, or his manservant or maidservant, his ox or donkey, or anything that belongs to your neighbor." (Exodus 20:17)

   b. Resist the world's view that claims we have to have things to be happy.
   c. Discontentment can cause us to toss aside __honor__ and integrity.

   Acts 5:1-10, Matthew 26:14,15; Matthew 27:5

   d. We have to make a choice to serve God or money.

8. **The Price of Greed**
   a. Over-commitment to ___*profit*___ can cause failure.

   Samuel 15:3, 9, 26

   b. When the desire for money becomes an obsession, nothing can satisfy.
   c. Greedy people may have everything, but they don't have a ___*clean*___ heart and a clear conscience.

Ordering your life according to His values and principles will make you successful by any measurement.

---

9. **Living without Distractions**
   a. Don't be ___*preoccupied*___ with creating great gain.

   "So do not worry, saying, 'What shall we eat?' or 'What shall we drink?' or 'What shall we wear?' For the pagans run after all these things and your heavenly Father knows that you need them. But seek first His kingdom and His righteousness, and all these things will be given to you as well. Therefore do not worry about tomorrow, for tomorrow will worry about itself. Each day has enough trouble of its own." (Matthew 6:31-33)

   "I am not saying this because I am in need, for I have learned to be content whatever the circumstances. I know what it is to be in need, and I know what it is to have plenty. I have learned the secret of being content in any and every situation, whether well fed or hungry, whether living in plenty or in want." (Philippians 4:11,12)

   b. Be thankful and don't worry about every little thing.
   c. Use money as a ___*tool*___, not a means to accumulate material goods.
   d. Not money, but spiritual treasures accumulated on earth will pass with us to eternity.
   e. Knowing Christ is to be ___*eternally*___ wealthy.

Lesson 1: Money in God's Economy

10. Values and Principles
   a. Our walk in God's economic world is faith-based.
   b. God takes __action__ in our lives for our ultimate benefit.
   c. As stewards, we are required to give a faithful account for what God has entrusted to us.

11. Our Natural Economy
Naturally, we experience debt, bankruptcy, recession, depression and other financial crises, but in God's __economy__, these do not exist.

12. God's Supernatural Provision
   a. God turns __little__ into much.

   Matthew 14:19-21

   b. The level of our blessing may depend on the level of our faith.

   II Kings 4:1-7

Money is a tool, not a treasure.

---

13. Wealthy People of the Bible
   a. There is no harm in __possessing__ riches. (Joseph of Arimathea, Barnabas, Abraham, Solomon)
   b. Harm comes when __riches__ possess us.

   "Now listen, you rich people, weep and wail because of the misery that is coming upon you. Your wealth has rotted, and moths have eaten your clothes. Your gold and silver are corroded. Their corrosion will testify against you and eat your flesh like fire. You have hoarded wealth in the last days. Look! The wages you failed to pay the workmen who mowed your fields are crying out against you. The cries of

the harvesters have reached the ears of the Lord Almighty. You have lived on earth in luxury and self-indulgence. You have fattened yourselves in the day of slaughter." (James 5:1-3)*

c. Wealth is short-lived.

"Do not store up for yourselves treasures on earth, where moth and rust destroy, and where thieves break in and steal. But store up for yourselves treasures in heaven, where moth and rust do not destroy, and where thieves do not break in and steal. For where your treasure is, there your heart will be also." (Matthew 6:19-21)

Be a conduit, not a dam. It is not about what we have, but what has us.

---

14. The Stewardship of Possessions

"But godliness with contentment is great gain. For we brought nothing into the world, and we can take nothing out of it. But if we have food and clothing, we will be content with that. People who want to get rich fall into temptation and a trap and into many foolish and harmful desires that plunge men into ruin and destruction. For the love of money is a root of all kinds of evil. Some people, eager for money, have wandered from the faith and pierced themselves with many griefs." (I Timothy 6:6-10)

a. The stewardship of material __goods__ comes to grips with the question of ownership.

"Whoever can be trusted with very little can also be trusted with much, and whoever is dishonest with very little will also be dishonest with much. So if you have not been trustworthy in handling worldly wealth, who will trust you with true riches? And if you have not been trustworthy with someone else's property, who will give you property of your own? No servant can serve two masters. Either he will hate the one and love the other, or he will be devoted to the one and despise the other. You cannot serve both God and Money." (Luke 16:11-13)

b. What we care about we __invest__ in.

   II Corinthians 8:4-7

c. Stewardship means recognizing your obligation to God because of Calvary.

15. Our Position as Trustee
   a. Placing __God__ first

   "But seek first his kingdom and his righteousness, and all these things will be given to you as well." (Matthew 6:33)

   b. Trusting God's Provision
   c. God's __desire__ to bless

   "Delight yourself in the LORD and he will give you the desires of your heart." (Psalms 37:4)

16. Responsible with Finances
   a. God is the __owner__ so we must be responsible.

   Deuteronomy 8:18

   b. Our time on earth is short and then we go to an eternal destination.

   "But store up for yourselves treasures in heaven, where moth and rust do not destroy, and where thieves do not break in and steal. For where your treasure is, there your heart will be also." (Matthew 6:20,21)

   c. Cherish __eternal__ treasure.

NOTES

Lesson 1: Money in God's Economy

STUDENT RESPONSE
IMPROVEMENT ACTION PLAN

What I need to change:_____

What? I define my goal as this achievable result. What will be my final outcome?

My Answer:_____

_____

Why? This is why I need to accomplish my goal.

My Answer:_____

_____

Who? Who will be involved in making me successful?

My Answer:_____

_____

Where? Where will I get started? In what area will I begin?

My Answer:_____

_____

How? How will I accomplish what I want to achieve? How will I measure my progress?

My Answer:_____

_____

When? When will I begin working on achieving this goal?

My Answer:_____

_____

Lesson Two

The Cycle of Money

All streams flow into the sea, yet the sea is never full.
To the place the streams come from, there they return again.
ECCLESIASTES 1:7

Then God said, "Let the land produce vegetation; seed-bearing plants and
trees on the land that bear fruit with seed in it,
according to their various kinds."
GENESIS 1:11

Make money your God, and it will plague you like the devil.
HENRY FIELDING

Fame is a vapor, popularity is an accident, money takes wings,
those who cheer you today may curse you tomorrow.
The only thing that endures is character.
HORACE GREELEY

Lesson Two

THE CYCLE OF MONEY

1. **The Cycle of Nature**
   a. The Seed Cycle
   b. The __Water__ Cycle
      i) Precipitation can become useful groundwater.
      ii) Precipitation can also be stored.

2. **The Cycle of Money**
   a. When __increase__ comes our way, we should use it for our needs and for the good of others.
   b. The measure we give determines the measure we receive.

   "Give, and it shall be given you; good measure, pressed down, and shaken together, and running over, shall men give into your bosom. For with the same measure that ye mete withal it shall be measured to you again." (Luke 6:38, KJV)

   c. God multiplies and __enriches__ the resources of the giver.

   II Corinthians 9:6-15

3. **The Significance of Giving**

   "Lay not up for yourselves treasures upon earth, where moth and rust doth corrupt, and where thieves break through and steal: But lay up for yourselves treasures in heaven, where neither moth nor rust doth corrupt, and where thieves do not break through nor steal: For where your treasure is, there will your heart be also." (Matthew 6:19-21, KJV)

   a. The wealthy have an __obligation__ to the needy.
   b. Unused wealth will get you nowhere.

"*Your wealth has rotted, and moths have eaten your clothes. Your gold and silver are corroded. Their corrosion will testify against you.*" (James 5:2,3a)

    c. All __wealth__ can be destroyed.

4. **The Law of Sowing and Reaping**
   a. The seed we __plant__ is the same kind we will reap: seed of its kind.
   b. We determine the size of the harvest at the time of planting.

   II Corinthians 9:6,8,11

   c. We will __always__ have a harvest.

   Malachi 3:10, Galatians 6:9

Giving money is significant to God because giving money is a way to give of yourself.

---

    d. You usually reap later than you sow.
    e. We always __reap__ more than we plant.

   Matthew 13:8

    f. There is a season for planting and a season for harvesting.

   Ecclesiastes 3:1,2

    g. Seed can be sown secretly, but the __harvest__ ¬will be viewed by many.
    h. We are responsible to sow, but God is responsible for bringing the harvest.

5. **Principles of Personal Finance**
   a. God __owns__ everything.
      i) Understanding this puts you in a position to prosper as you partner with God.

"The earth is the Lord's, and everything in it, the world, and all who live in it." (Psalms 24:1)

"'The silver is mine and the gold is mine,' declares the LORD Almighty." (Haggai 2:8)

"For every animal of the forest is mine, and the cattle on a thousand hills. I know every bird in the mountains, and the creatures of the field are mine." (Psalms 50:10,11)

    ii)   God gives you the ability to earn a living.

The law of living is giving. If money is to be useful, it must be used.

---

b.   How __*money*__ Is Obtained
  - i)   The manner in which finances are acquired and disbursed must be based on sound moral guidelines.
  - ii)   With access to resources comes __*accountability*__ – you must prove yourself a good steward.
  - iii)   Our life's stewardship should reflect God's interest in all that He has trusted us with.

Genesis 1:26, 2:15

  - iv)   The value system of one's heart is __*exposed*__ by one's relationship to money and material things.

Matthew 19:16-22

  - v)   Spend your time investing in things of eternal nature.
  - vi)   Those who "have everything", but not a loving family, a clean heart, honor, and the __*blessing*__ of God are miserable.

Biblical Principles for Financial Success   Teacher Workbook

      vii) Leaving all scruples and morals for the sake of money is foolish.
      viii) God is concerned about our ____actions____ and motives.
  c. How Money Is Disbursed
     i) Not money, but our attitude about it may be wrong.

"People who want to get rich fall into temptation and a trap and into many foolish and harmful desires..." (I Timothy 6:9)

If God cannot trust you with $100 now, how can He trust you with $1,000 or $100,000?

---

     ii) We will be blessed if we use the monetary blessings God has given us to finance His cause and ____further____ His kingdom.

"For we brought nothing into this world, and it is certain we can carry nothing out." (I Timothy 6:7)

"For in him we live and move and have our being." (Deuteronomy 8:18)

"But remember the LORD your God, for it is He who gives you the ability to produce wealth..." (Acts 17:28)

"For every living soul belongs to me." (Ezekiel 18:4)

"Therefore, I urge you, brothers, in view of God's mercy, to offer your bodies as living sacrifices, holy and pleasing to God." (Romans 12:1)

"Know that the LORD is God. It is he who made us, and we are his; we are his people, the sheep of his pasture." (Psalms 100:3)

"You are not your own; you were bought at a price. Therefore honor God with your body." (I Corinthians 6:19-20)

iii) Don't try to figure out how little you can give; give God __everything__ and ask how much you should keep.

d. How Money Is Contributed

    i) Your use of money must not violate the laws of the land or the principles of God's Word.

    ii) Our motives and __priorities__ must reflect, "God first, me last."

"Seek ye first the kingdom of God, and his righteousness; and all these things shall be added unto you." (Matthew 6:33)

    iii) Though ungodly men and women achieve prosperity apart from God, they can never achieve the deep, settled peace that comes from God.

Psalms 73:3, Proverbs 13:22

    iv) Giving is the __trigger__ for financial miracles.

Luke 6:38, II Corinthians 9:6

In business, when you partner with God, He not only will bless it, He will let you enjoy prosperity.

NOTES

Lesson 2: The Cycle of Money

STUDENT RESPONSE
IMPROVEMENT ACTION PLAN

What I need to change: _____

What? I define my goal as this achievable result. What will be my final outcome?

My Answer: _____

_____

Why? This is why I need to accomplish my goal.

My Answer: _____

_____

Who? Who will be involved in making me successful?

My Answer: _____

_____

Where? Where will I get started? In what area will I begin?

My Answer: _____

_____

How? How will I accomplish what I want to achieve? How will I measure my progress?

My Answer: _____

_____

When? When will I begin working on achieving this goal?

My Answer: _____

_____

Lesson Three

THE BLESSING OF GIVING

But just as you excel in everything—in faith, in speech, in knowledge, in complete
earnestness and in your love for us—see that you also excel in this grace of giving.
II CORINTHIANS 8:7

...remembering the words the Lord Jesus himself said: "It is more blessed
to give than to receive."
ACTS 20:35

Give, and it will be given to you. A good measure, pressed down, shaken together and
running over, will be poured into your lap. For with the measure you use,
it will be measured to you.
LUKE 6:38

Lesson Three

THE BLESSING OF GIVING

1. **God's Perspective**
   Our wealth does not come from what we grab in life, but from what we __give__ in life.

2. **A Blessing or a Curse**

   James 5:1-3

3. **Ultimate Ownership**
   You own __nothing__ and God owns everything.

4. **A God-Given Ability**
   God gives you the __ability__ to earn.

   "But remember the LORD your God, for it is he who gives you the ability to produce wealth…" (Deuteronomy 8:18)

   "The earth is the LORD's, and everything in it, the world, and all who live in it." (Psalms 24:1)

   "For every animal of the forest is mine, and the cattle on a thousand hills. I know every bird in the mountains, and the creatures of the field are mine." (Psalms 50:10,11)

   "Know that the LORD is God. It is he who made us, and we are his; we are his people, the sheep of his pasture." (Psalms 100:3)

   "For every living soul belongs to me." (Ezekiel 18:4)

"'The silver is mine and the gold is mine,' declares the LORD Almighty." (Haggai 2:8)

"For in him we live and move and have our being." (Acts 17:28)

"Therefore, I urge you, brothers, in view of God's mercy, to offer your bodies as living sacrifices, holy and pleasing to God." (Romans 12:1)

5. **We Are Not Our Own**
   Because you ___belong___ to God, all you have belongs to Him.

   "You are not your own; you were bought at a price. Therefore honor God with your body." (I Corinthians 6:19-20)

There is no harm in possessing riches as long as the riches do not possess you.

---

6. **The Joy of Giving**
   When God is our ___source___, our well will not run dry and we will be able to.

   "Will a man rob God? Yet you rob me. But you ask, 'How do we rob you?' In tithes and offerings. You are under a curse— the whole nation of you— because you are robbing me. Bring the whole tithe into the storehouse, that there may be food in my house. Test me in this," says the LORD Almighty, "and see if I will not throw open the floodgates of heaven and pour out so much blessing that you will not have room enough for it. I will prevent pests from devouring your crops..."

   (Malachi 3:8-11)

   "One man gives freely, yet grows all the richer; another withholds what he should give, and only suffers want. A liberal man will be enriched, and one who waters will himself be watered." (Proverbs 11:24, RSV)

"Don't be deceived, my dear brothers. Every good and perfect gift is from above, coming down from the Father..." (James 1:16,17)

7. **Our Only Resource**
   God is the source of your ___abundant___ supply.

   "And my God shall supply all your need according to His riches..." (Philippians 4:19, NKJ)

Nothing happens in the economy of God until you give something away.

---

8. **Be Careful about Greed**
   Spiritual prosperity is more ___important___ than material prosperity.

   "Watch out! Be on your guard against all kinds of greed; a man's life does not consist in the abundance of his possessions." (Luke 12:15)

   "Beloved, I pray that you may prosper in all things and be in health, just as your soul prospers." (III John 2, NKJ)

   "As long as [King Uzziah] sought the LORD, God gave him success." (II Chronicles 26:5)

   "Do not let this Book of the Law depart from your mouth; meditate on it day and night, so that you may be careful to do everything written in it. Then you will be prosperous and successful." (Joshua 1:8)

9. **The Blessing of Tithing**
   a. God is training us to be faithful ___stewards___ in handling money.
   b. Tithing is commanded.

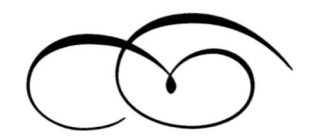

Never measure generosity by what you give,
but by what you have left.
FULTON SHEEN

When it come to giving until it hurts, most people
have a very low threshold of pain.
ANONYMOUS

Never worry about numbers. Help one person at a time,
and always start with the person nearest you.
MOTHER TERESA

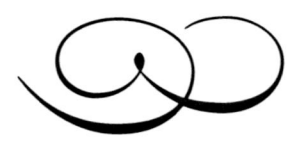

"Bring ye all the tithes into the storehouse." (Malachi 3:10)

"Let every one of you lay by him in store, as God hath prospered him." (I Corinthians 16:2)

   c. Abraham __tithed__ before the law of Moses.

   Genesis 14:11-20

   d. The New Testament recounts the first tithe.

   Hebrews 7:1-19

   e. A __tithe__ is a tenth.

10. First Fruits
Tithing does away with "hit and miss" methods of giving.

11. Jesus Christ Endorsed Tithing.

Luke 18:22

Jesus Himself __tithed__; we know this because only tithers were allowed into the homes of Pharisees.

Luke 11:37

12. Jesus Christ Approved the Tenth.

Matthew 23:23, Matthew 22:21

13. Solomon Taught Tithing.

"Honour the LORD with thy substance, and with the firstfruits of all thine increase: So shall thy barns be filled with plenty, and thy presses shall burst out with new wine." (Proverbs 3:9-10, KJV)

14. Beyond the Tithe
Giving is __seed__ and God will see that we reap a harvest.

"Be not deceived; God is not mocked: for whatsoever a man soweth, that shall he also reap." (Galatians 6:7, KJV)

"Bring ye all the tithes into the storehouse, that there may be meat in mine house, and prove me now herewith, saith the LORD of hosts, if I will not open you the windows of heaven, and pour you out a blessing, that there shall not be room enough to receive it." (Malachi 3:10)

15. Giving Expresses Our Love.

"Each man should give what he has decided in his heart to give, not reluctantly or under compulsion, for God loves a cheerful giver." (II Corinthians 9:7)

"If I give all I possess to the poor and surrender my body to the flames, but have not love, I gain nothing." (I Corinthians 13:3)

The only way to get our treasures into heaven is to put them into something that is going to heaven.

---

16. Giving Freely

A giving person gives with a spirit of genuine __generosity__. When he or she receives, it is a totally unexpected blessing.

"Good will come to him who is generous.... He has scattered abroad his gifts to the poor, his righteousness endures forever; his horn will be lifted high in honor." (Psalms 112:5,9)

"...without expecting to get anything back. Then your reward will be great..." (Luke 6:35)

"It is more blessed to give than to receive." (Acts 20:35, KJV)

17. Giving and Obedience
Generous giving comes from a humble and loving heart.

18. Bountiful Giving
When you give, give bountifully and generously with pure motives.

Freely giving protects us from the pitfalls of greed and materialism.

NOTES

Lesson 3: The Blessing of Giving

STUDENT RESPONSE
IMPROVEMENT ACTION PLAN

What I need to change:_____

What? I define my goal as this achievable result. What will be my final outcome?

My Answer:_____

_____

Why? This is why I need to accomplish my goal.

My Answer:_____

_____

Who? Who will be involved in making me successful?

My Answer:_____

_____

Where? Where will I get started? In what area will I begin?

My Answer:_____

_____

How? How will I accomplish what I want to achieve? How will I measure my progress?

My Answer:_____

_____

When? When will I begin working on achieving this goal?

My Answer:_____

_____

NOTES

Module 2

Man's Stewardship

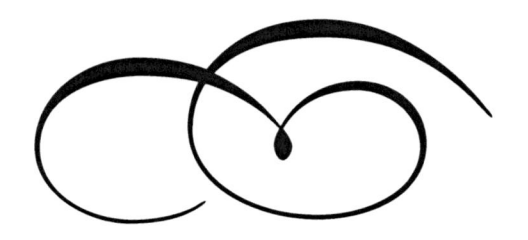

Lesson Four

Principles of a Blessed Person

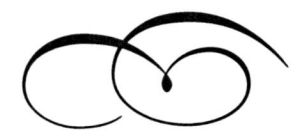

The LORD will open the heavens, the storehouse of His bounty,
to send rain on your land in season and to bless all the work of your hands.
You will lend to many nations but will borrow from none.
DEUTERONOMY 28:12

If a person gets his attitude toward money straight,
it will help straighten out almost every other area of his life.
Tell me what you think about money and I can tell you
what you think about God, for these two are closely related.
A man's heart is closer to his wallet than almost anything else.
BILLY GRAHAM

I am a little pencil in the hand of a writing God
who is sending a love letter to the world.
MOTHER TERESA

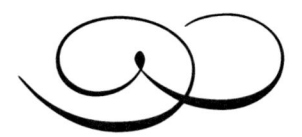

Lesson Four

PRINCIPLES OF A BLESSED PERSON

1. **The Heart Attitude**
   The blessed person gives of his or her resources freely, _cheerfully_, and out of genuine appreciation to God.

2. **Money Cannot Buy Happiness.**
   "Then he said to them, 'Watch out! Be on your guard against all kinds of greed; a man's life does not consist in the abundance of his possessions.'" (Luke 12:15)

Are we a conduit, or do we stop the stream of God's favor?

---

3. **Principles of Blessing**
   - The principle of knowing that God _owns_ it all (Haggai 2:8-9, I Corinthians 4:2, Psalms 50:10, II Corinthians 9:7)
   - The principle of giving from the top (Genesis 14:20, Proverbs 3:9)
   - The principle of supernatural provision (I Kings 17:14-16)
   - The principle of being _proactive_ (Matthew 17:27, Ecclesiastes 9:11, Hebrews 12:1,2, Proverbs 21:5)
   - The principle of knowing how to be content (I Timothy 6:8-9)
   - The principle of resisting world views (Romans 12:2)
   - The principle of _plenty_ left over (II Corinthians 9:8-9)
   - The principle of feeding the local house (Malachi 3:10)

Biblical Principles for Financial Success   Teacher Workbook

- The principle of obedience (Malachi 3:10)
- The principle of __advance__ preparation (Genesis 41:47-49)
- The principle of honesty (Malachi 3:8,10, Matthew 6:33)
- The principle of __temporary__ possessions (I Timothy 6:7-8)

> ### We must resist the world's view of wealth, happiness and possessions. We do not have to have it all!

- The principle of giving to the needy (I John 3:17)
- The principle of right attitudes (II Corinthians 9:6-9)
- The principle of __systematic__ giving (I Corinthians 16:2-3)
- The principle of giving freely (Matthew 10:8)
- The principle of never withholding (Proverbs 11:24-28, I Kings 17)
- The principle of the tenth (Genesis 28:20-22)
- The principle of increased measure (Luke 6:38)
- The principle of __learning__ prosperity (Joshua 1:8-9)
- The principle of supply (Philippians 4:18-20)

> ### Giving starts with tithing.

- The principle of __sacrificial__ giving (Mark 12:41-44)
- The principle of heart decisions (II Corinthians 9:7)
- The principle of equal giving (II Corinthians 8:10-12)
- The principle of __faithfulness__ (I Corinthians 4:2-3, Deuteronomy 5:32)

Lesson 4: Principles of a Blessed Person

- The principle of laying up treasures (I Timothy 6:19)
- The principle of the sluggard lifestyle (Proverbs 24:30-34, Proverbs 12:27)
- The principle of ___working___ diligently (Proverbs 6:6-11, Proverbs 22:29)
- The principle of brotherhood (I John 3:17, Romans 12:13)
- The principle of giving out of your poverty (II Corinthians 8:1-5)
- The principle of giving gifts (II Corinthians 9:9)
- The principle of ___refreshing___ (Proverbs 11:25)
- The principle of misplaced trust (Proverbs 11:28)
- The principle of giving special gifts (Deuteronomy 12:11-12)
- The principle of ___understanding___ the greater blessing (Acts 20:34-35)
- The principle of placing our treasure (Matthew 6:20-21)
- The principle of generous giving (II Corinthians 8:2)
- The principle of ___contentment___ (I Timothy 6:6-7)

Stewardship is the management of our entire lives, all that we have and all that we are.

- The principle of leaving it all behind (I Timothy 6:7)
- The principle of foolish desires (I Timothy 6:9-10)
- The principle of not loving money (I Timothy 6:10)
- The principle of being humble (I Timothy 6:17)
- The principle of ___hope___ in God (I Timothy 6:17-18)
- The principle of sharing (I Timothy 6:18)
- The principle of ___guarding___ (I Timothy 6:20)
- The principle of sacrifice (Luke 21:4)
- The principle of placing your needs last (I Kings 17:9-16)
- The principle of ___blessing___ others (Genesis 12:2-3)

- The principle of open floodgates (Malachi 3:10)
- The principle of excess blessing (Malachi 3:10)
- The principle of __financial__ protection (Malachi 3:11-12)
- The principle of transparent blessing (Malachi 3:12)

You need to understand your calling and purpose in life and set out objectives that will allow you to live that fulfilled life.

- The principle of first fruits (Proverbs 3:9)
- The principle of __full__ barns (Proverbs 3:10)
- The principle of the first born (Exodus 13:1-2)
- The principle of God as Master (Matthew 6:24)
- The principle of __trusting__ God (Matthew 6:34)
- The principle of resisting temptation (Matthew 4:8-11)
- The principle of a pure heart (Matthew 5:8)
- The principle of showing mercy (Matthew 5:7)
- The principle of __right__ relationships (Matthew 5:23-24)
- The principle of correct giving (Matthew 6:2)

Money and possessions last, at best, only a lifetime. At worst, they could be gone tomorrow.

- The principle of understanding greed (Luke 12:16-19)
- The principle of __providing__ for family (I Timothy 5:8)

Lesson 4: Principles of a Blessed Person

- The principle of lending to the Lord (Proverbs 19:17)
- The principle of righteous giving (Proverbs 21:26)
- The principle of lacking nothing (Proverbs 28:27)
- The principle of sharing coats (Luke 3:11)
- The principle of __diligence__ in business (Romans 12:11-12)
- The principle of a cheerful giver (II Corinthians 9:7)
- The principle of sowing bountifully (II Corinthians 9:6)
- The principle of __enjoying__ all things (I Timothy 6:17)
- The principle of honoring the Lord (Proverbs 3:9)
- The principle of finding God's provision (Matthew 17:27)
- The principle of __freedom__ from the love of money (Hebrews 13:4-5)
- The principle of knowing the Source (I Chronicles 29:10-12)
- The principle of the ultimate gift (John 3:16, Romans 8:31-33)

NOTES

Lesson 4: Principles of a Blessed Person

STUDENT RESPONSE

IMPROVEMENT ACTION PLAN

What I need to change:_____

What? I define my goal as this achievable result. What will be my final outcome?

My Answer:_____

_____

Why? This is why I need to accomplish my goal.

My Answer:_____

_____

Who? Who will be involved in making me successful?

My Answer:_____

_____

Where? Where will I get started? In what area will I begin?

My Answer:_____

_____

How? How will I accomplish what I want to achieve? How will I measure my progress?

My Answer:_____

_____

When? When will I begin working on achieving this goal?

My Answer:_____

_____

Lesson Five

PERSONA OF A STEWARD

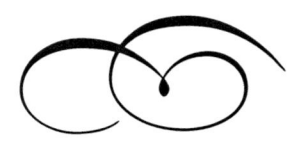

Having started the ball rolling so enthusiastically, you should carry this project through to completion just as gladly, giving whatever you can out of whatever you have. Let your enthusiastic idea at the start be equaled by your realistic action now.
II CORINTHIANS 8:11 (TLB)

The only gift is a portion of thyself.
RALPH WALDO EMERSON

I've seen you stalking the malls, walking the aisles,
searching for that extra-special gift. Stashing away a few dolars a month
to buy him some lizard-skin boots; staring at a thousand rings
to find her the best diamond; staying up all night Christmas Eve,
assembling the new bicycle. Why do you do it?
So the eyes will pop, the jaw will drop. To hear those words of disbelief:
"You did this for me?" And that is why God did it.
Next time a sunrise steals your breath
or a meadow of flowers leaves you speechless, remain that way.
Say nothing, and listen as heaven whispers,
"Do you like it? I did it just for you."
MAX LUCADO, THE GREAT HOUSE OF GOD (WORD)

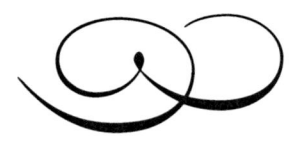

Lesson Five

PERSONA OF A STEWARD

1. **Introduction**
   a. Worldly priorities are to surround oneself with all the comforts the world has to offer, but this is not the __scriptural__ perspective.

   "Praise be to the God and Father of our Lord Jesus Christ, the Father of compassion and the God of all comfort, who comforts us in all our troubles, so that we can comfort those in any trouble with the comfort we ourselves have received from God. For just as the sufferings of Christ flow over into our lives, so also through Christ our comfort overflows. If we are distressed, it is for your comfort and salvation; if we are comforted, it is for your comfort, which produces in you patient endurance of the same sufferings we suffer. And our hope for you is firm, because we know that just as you share in our sufferings, so also you share in our comfort." (II Corinthians 1:3-7)

   b. The Bible teaches stewardship, that our __possessions__ are not ours, but God's, and they have been given to us for a purpose.

   Mark 10:17-22

2. **Stewardship in Scripture**

   Genesis 1:28, Matthew 10:8

3. **Old Testament Stewardship**
   The steward of the Old Testament was given the task of __overseeing__ another's possessions or household. It was the number one servant, possessing a place of authority and accountability. The steward would later become the heir.

   Genesis 15:2, Genesis 24

4. **New Testament Stewardship**

Good stewards were rewarded with increased *responsibility* and income, but a poor steward was disgraced or fired. A steward is held accountable.

Luke 16:1-13

5. **A Steward's Character**
   Honest and Faithful

   "Moreover it is required in stewards, that a man be found faithful." (1 Corinthians 4:2, KJV)

The astute businessperson looks ahead and plans for the future. He or she manages money so as to provide benefits not only for the present, but for the future.

---

6. **Integrity Issues**
   Integrity is "being *complete*, unimpaired, perfect condition, of sound moral principle, uprightness." (*Webster's Dictionary*)

   "Better is the poor that walketh in his integrity, than he that is perverse in his lips, and is a fool." (Proverbs 19:1, KJV)

7. **The Whole Picture**
   God is interested in the stewardship of not only our finances, but our *entire* life.

8. **Planning Ahead**

   "I tell you, use worldly wealth to gain friends for yourselves, so that when it is gone, you will be welcomed into eternal dwellings." (Luke 16:9)

9. **Acknowledging God**
   God owns the earth; *everything* comes from Him.

Lesson 5: Persona of a Steward

1 Chronicles 29:13,14, Exodus 9:29, Isaiah 66:1,2, Acts 7:49,50, II Kings 19:15, Nehemiah 9:6, Jeremiah 27:5, Hebrews 1:10, Acts 17:24, Job 12:9-10, Psalm 89:11, Psalm 95:3-5, Daniel 4:17, John 19:11, Rev 4:11

10. **God in Control**

    Romans 12:1

What does God already own that you are trying to keep absolute control over by refusing to acknowledge God's ownership?

---

11. **Faithfulness**
    Be faithful to ____*obey*____ the Lord when He asks something of you.

    Deuteronomy 5:32

12. **Oversight**
    When we are faithful, God allows us to be overseers of His property.

    "For every beast of the forest is mine, and the cattle upon a thousand hills. I know all the fowls of the mountains: and the wild beasts of the field are mine." (Psalm 50:10,11, KJV)

13. **Reflection**
    How we ____*manage*____ our possessions must reflect God's interest.

    Genesis 1:26, 2:15

14. **Caring for God's Gifts**

15. **Reliability**

16. **Managing Our Possessions**

    "So if you have not been trustworthy in handling worldly wealth, who will trust you with true riches?" (Luke 16:11)

    "His divine power has given us everything we need for life and godliness..." (2 Peter 1:3)

Give more than is required. Go the second mile. And the third and fourth.

---

17. **Unlimited Resources**

18. **Financial Control**

19. **Dominion over Creation**
    God gave us authority over creation, but we must __*exercise*__ it through work.

    "In the sweat of thy face shalt thou eat bread, till thou return unto the ground..." (Genesis 3:19, KJV)

    "For even when we were with you, this we commanded you, that if any would not work, neither should he eat." (II Thessalonians 3:10, KJV)

20. **Use of Personal Resources**

    Matthew 25:14-30

21. **Working Hard**

Lesson 5: Persona of a Steward

"Go to the ant, you sluggard; consider its ways and be wise! It has no commander, no overseer or ruler, yet it stores its provisions in summer and gathers its food at harvest. How long will you lie there, you sluggard? When will you get up from your sleep? A little sleep, a little slumber, a little folding of the hands to rest-- and poverty will come on you like a bandit and scarcity like an armed man." (Proverbs 6:6-11)

"Make it your ambition to lead a quiet life, to mind your own business and to work with your hands, just as we told you, so that your daily life may win the respect of outsiders and so that you will not be dependent on anybody." (I Thessalonians 4:11,12)

"Lazy hands make a man poor, but diligent hands bring wealth. He who gathers crops in summer is a wise son, but he who sleeps during harvest is a disgraceful son" (Proverbs 10:4,5)

"Do you see a man skilled in his work? He will serve before kings; he will not serve before obscure men." (Proverbs 22:29)

"Whatever your hand finds to do, do it with all your might..." (Ecclesiastes 9:10)

"A sluggard does not plow in season; so at harvest time he looks but finds nothing." (Proverbs 20:4)

22. The Virtue of Diligence

23. Prosperous and Successful

When we apply biblical instruction, work hard and lead a __disciplined__ lifestyle, we will experience success in life.

24. Productive Stewardship

John 15:1-5

25. Developing God's Gifts

a. Idleness and __laziness__ will be judged.

Ecclesiastes 10:18

b. We will give an account on judgment day.

Matthew 12:36

c. We can make good use of the ___*gift*___ of time.

Ephesians 5:16

d. We are responsible for the development of God's gifts in us.

Matthew 25

Lesson 5: Persona of a Steward

STUDENT RESPONSE
IMPROVEMENT ACTION PLAN

What I need to change:_____

What? I define my goal as this achievable result. What will be my final outcome?

My Answer:_____

_____

Why? This is why I need to accomplish my goal.

My Answer:_____

_____

Who? Who will be involved in making me successful?

My Answer:_____

_____

Where? Where will I get started? In what area will I begin?

My Answer:_____

_____

How? How will I accomplish what I want to achieve? How will I measure my progress?

My Answer:_____

_____

When? When will I begin working on achieving this goal?

My Answer:_____

_____

Lesson Six

DISCIPLINES OF A STEWARD

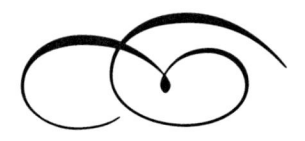

Redeeming the time, because the days are evil.
EPHESIANS 5:16 (KJV)

Go to the ant, you sluggard; consider its ways and be wise!
It has no commander, no overseer or ruler,
yet it stores its provisions in summer and gathers
its food at harvest. How long will you lie there, you sluggard?
When will you get up from your sleep? A little sleep,
a little slumber, a little folding of the hands
to rest—and poverty will come on you
like a bandit and scarcity like an armed man.
PROVERBS 6:6-11

Remember that time is money.
BENJAMIN FRANKLIN

Lesson Six

DISCIPLINES OF A STEWARD

1. **God's Gift of Time**
   a. As stewards, we must use time __wisely__ and to our advantage in fulfilling our destiny.
   b. Time management takes self-control, perseverance and self-discipline, but this investment pays high dividends.
   c. We should consider budgeting and __investing__ our time, much as we do our finances.
   d. How we use our time counts.

2. **The Investment of Time**
   a. To __invest__ is to use something in such a way as to bring future benefits.
   b. Time carefully planned and invested will rarely be wasted.

3. **The Value of Time**
   Prioritize your time so that __important__ matters will not be forgotten or left out.

4. **The Purpose of Time**
   It is not how much you do that counts, but how much has __purpose__ and lasting benefit.

5. **The Bank of Time**
   Our time is an __account__ that is replenished and then emptied daily.

6. **The Stewardship of Time**
   a. Plan your work.
   b. List your tasks.
   c. Develop a __regular__ work schedule.

d. Do related jobs together.
   e. Learn to rest creatively.

7. **The Control of Time**
   Develop habits that put you in ___control___ of your time.

   "Before the mountains were born or you brought forth the earth and the world, from everlasting to everlasting you are God." (Psalms 90:2)

   "For a thousand years in your sight are like a day that has just gone by, or like a watch in the night." (Psalms 90:4)

   "The length of our days is seventy years—or eighty, if we have the strength; yet their span is but trouble and sorrow, for they quickly pass, and we fly away." (Psalms 90:10)

   "Teach us to number our days aright, that we may gain a heart of wisdom." (Psalms 90:12)

Knowledge is advantageous, skill is indispensable, experience is invaluable, communication is fundamental, enthusiasm is beneficial, attitude is essential—but personal discipline determines the level of your achievement.

---

8. **God's Gift of Communication**

   "But to do good, and to communicate forget not: for with such sacrifices God is well pleased." (Hebrews 13:16, KJV)

   "And he said unto them, What manner of communications are these that ye have one to another, as ye walk, and are sad." (Luke 24:17, KJV)

"But let your communication be, Yea, yea; Nay, nay: for whatsoever is more than these cometh of evil." (Matthew 5:37, KJV)

"Let no corrupt communication proceed out of your mouth, but that which is good to the use of edifying, that it may minister grace unto the hearers." (Ephesians 4:29, KJV)

"But now ye also put off all these; anger, wrath, malice, blasphemy, filthy communication out of your mouth." (Colossians 3:8, KJV)

"Be not deceived: evil communications corrupt good manners." (I Corinthians 15:33, KJV)

9. **The Stewardship of Communication**
   Our ability to _communicate_ with others is one of God's greatest gifts and often, one of our greatest challenges.

10. **Defining Communication**
    (from *Strong's Greek/Hebrew Dictionary* and *Vine's Expository Dictionary of Biblical Words*)
    a. Communication
       i. Partnership, _participation_, social intercourse, communication, communion and fellowship

       Hebrews 13:16, Philemon 6

       ii. A spoken word, communication, speech

       Luke 24:17, Matthew 5:37, Ephesians 4:29, Colossians 3:8

    b. To Communicate
       i. To have a share in, give a share to, _share_ with, communicate, have fellowship with

       Romans 15:27, 1 Timothy 5:22, Hebrews 2:14, I Peter 4:13, II John 11, Romans 12:13, Galatians 6:6

Biblical Principles for Financial Success   Teacher Workbook

      ii. To share together with, communicate with, partake of, share with others to meet needs

Philippians 4:14, Ephesians 5:11, Revelation 18:4

  c. Communicative: Apt/ __ready__ to Communicate

1 Timothy 6:18

11. The Cycle of Communication
Communication is the sending and receiving of information among people.
   a. What You __mean__ to Say
   b. What You Really Say
   c. What the Other Person Hears
   d. What the Other Person __thinks__ (S)He Heard
   e. What the Other Person Says about What You Said
   f. What You Think the Other Person __said__ about What You Said

12. Communication Difficulties
   a. Words mean different things to different people.
   b. Learn to be __objective__ and reflective in communication.

13. Benefits of Communication
   a. Careful listening is enormously beneficial.
   b. Identify the sender's __main__ idea by keeping your own ideas in the background.
   c. Concentrate on what the sender is saying.

14. Communication and Emotion
   a. Delay __evaluation__ of the message until after it is completed.
   b. Do not reject what you hear as too familiar, unfamiliar or trivial.
   c. Pay __attention__ not only to the words, but also what is being communicated in other ways.
   d. Do not formulate arguments against the sender's ideas before you fully understand them.

15. **Maximizing Communication**
    a. Ignore _uncomfortable_ surroundings.
    b. Do not refuse to listen to difficult or complicated information.

16. **Communication Connections**
    a. Look for points of agreement and _common_ points of interest.
    b. Words like "but" and "you" can inhibit good conversation.

17. **Styles of Communication**
    a. Your style of communication should have a positive effect on others.
    b. Try to make most of your communication _positive_ for others.
    c. Learn to put others at ease.

18. **Partners in Communication**
    Treat communication like a _contract_ between two or more individuals.

19. **Positive Communication**
    a. Choose positive words to make positive _reception_ as easy as possible.
    b. Try not to use generalizations.

20. **Communication Styles**
    a. Be aware of _negative_ communication behaviors or styles.
    b. Develop positive communication behaviors or styles.

21. **Conclusion**
    Our stewardship of time and _communication_ will have a direct effect on our finances.

Notes

STUDENT RESPONSE

IMPROVEMENT ACTION PLAN

What I need to change:_____

What? I define my goal as this achievable result. What will be my final outcome?

My Answer:_____

_____

Why? This is why I need to accomplish my goal.

My Answer:_____

_____

Who? Who will be involved in making me successful?

My Answer:_____

_____

Where? Where will I get started? In what area will I begin?

My Answer:_____

_____

How? How will I accomplish what I want to achieve? How will I measure my progress?

My Answer:_____

_____

When? When will I begin working on achieving this goal?

My Answer:_____

_____

NOTES

Module 3

Family Decisions

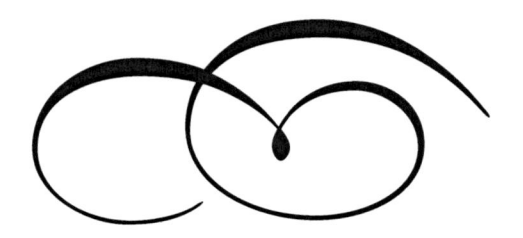

Lesson Seven

How to Make Wise Family Decisions

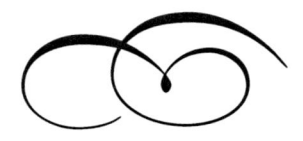

If only they were wise and would understand this and discern what their end will be!
DEUTERONOMY 32:29

I asked God for strength, that I might achieve.
I was made weak, that I might learn humbly to obey.
I asked for health, that I might do greater things.
I was given infirmity, that I might do better things.
I asked for riches, that I might be happy.
I was given poverty, that I might be wise.
I asked for power, that I might have the praise of men.
I was given weakness, that I might feel the need of God.
I asked for all things that I might enjy life.
I was given life, that I might enjoy all things.
I got nothing I asked for—but everything I had hoped for.
Almost despite myself, my unspoken prayers were answered.
I am, among all men, most richly blessed.
ANONYMOUS

Lesson Seven

HOW TO MAKE WISE FAMILY DECISIONS

1. **Introduction**
   a. Before thinking about long-term investment strategies, you must __understand__ the decision-making process.
   b. Decision-making is necessary to function effectively.
   c. Not all actions result from decisions, some result from habit.
   d. Money __expenditures__ can also result from habit or impulse.

2. **How a Decision Occurs**
   A decision occurs when a __judgment__ is consciously made and acted upon after weighing the facts and examining the alternatives and their outcomes. A decision can alter one's life as its effects continue on into the future.

Making decisions about financial affairs demands conscious attention to one's goals as well as to one's money.

---

3. **Characteristics of Decisions**
   a. Decisions are interrelated.
      Once a decision is made, it sets in motion a chain reaction of further decisions.
   b. Making a __choice__ involves risk.
      The outcome of a decision cannot always be predicted though we base it on all the facts available and upon the best advice.
   c. Decisions cause change.
      A change in __attitude__ may precede the decision.

d. Decisions require commitment.
   i. Without a serious commitment to one's goal, the drastic attitude and behavior changes – which are sometimes necessary – will hinder your _fulfillment_ of that goal.
   ii. Decisions make demands that require self-discipline.
e. Decisions involve cost.
   The cost of a financial decision can be difficult to accept and live with, because when money is used to reach your goals, there is less to use for other things.

4. **Three-Step Process**
   a. Seek _alternative_ solutions.
   b. Weigh the alternatives.
      Information must be gathered about costs; alternatives cannot be accurately judged unless enough is known about them.
   c. Make a choice.
      i. A choice is made based on personal goals and available resources.
      ii. The decision is put into action by _managing_ the necessary resources and activities.
      iii. Once the _decision_ has been made, no second-guessing!

The effectiveness of a decision is measured by whether or not it helps accomplish whatever one sets out to do.

---

5. **Effectiveness of a Decision**
   a. If a desired _outcome_ is being hindered, a decision may need to be re-evaluated.
   b. Decisions involving finance require specific knowledge and information.
   c. Decisions with long-term effects require _careful_ thought.

6. **Five Steps to Family Decisions**
    a. Recall past experience.
        Avoid making __mistakes__ you've made in the past.
    b. Keep financial records.
        When considering a new financial commitment, it is necessary to know how it may affect commitments that have already been made.
    c. Borrow __experience__ from people you know.
        When doing something for the first time, i.e. buying a house, investing for the future, ask someone who's already done it for advice.
    d. Look up specific information.
        Use the library and the Internet; background information and understanding are essential in choosing a course of action.
    e. Consult professionals and experts. __Review__ your decisions regularly and plan for difficulties you may face in the future.

NOTES

Lesson 7: How to Make Wise Family Decisions

STUDENT RESPONSE

IMPROVEMENT ACTION PLAN

What I need to change:_____

What? I define my goal as this achievable result. What will be my final outcome?

My Answer:_____

_____

Why? This is why I need to accomplish my goal.

My Answer:_____

_____

Who? Who will be involved in making me successful?

My Answer:_____

_____

Where? Where will I get started? In what area will I begin?

My Answer:_____

_____

How? How will I accomplish what I want to achieve? How will I measure my progress?

My Answer:_____

_____

When? When will I begin working on achieving this goal?

My Answer:_____

_____

Lesson Eight

FACING FINANCIAL CHALLENGES

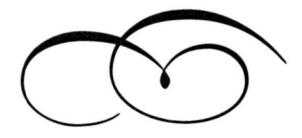

Give us counsel, render a decision. . . .
ISAIAH 16:3

Alas, how many, even among those who are called believers,
have plenty of all the necessities of life, and yet complain of poverty!
JOHN WESLEY

I do not pray for success. I ask for faithfulness.
MOTHER TERESA

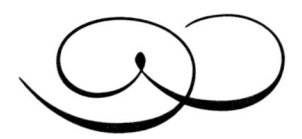

Lesson Eight

FACING FINANCIAL CHALLENGES

1. **Inevitable Challenges**
   Families are faced with many financial challenges and decision-making opportunities. Various resources can be used to solve these problems and to achieve individual family goals. Tackle one problem at a time. You will find __*satisfaction*__ in being in control of your financial life. Let's look at some steps toward solving financial challenges.

2. **Seeking Improvement**
   The process starts with __*recognizing*__ the difference between what is and what ought to be and then wanting to do something about it.

3. **Clarifying Goals**
   Prioritize your family's financial goals and rate them as to importance.

4. **Defining the Problem**
   State and carefully __*define*__ the obstacle(s) to each goal.

5. **Determining Resources**
   Examine what human and material resources are available; these all have potential to generate additional income to meet a specific family goal.

6. **Outlining Alternatives**
   a. Outline all alternatives and __*evaluate*__ each in terms of its outcome.
   b. Special information or assistance from experts should be obtained when a solution involves large amounts of money.

NOTES

Lesson 8: Facing Financial Challenges

STUDENT RESPONSE

IMPROVEMENT ACTION PLAN

What I need to change:_____

What? I define my goal as this achievable result. What will be my final outcome?

My Answer:_____

_____

Why? This is why I need to accomplish my goal.

My Answer:_____

_____

Who? Who will be involved in making me successful?

My Answer:_____

_____

Where? Where will I get started? In what area will I begin?

My Answer:_____

_____

How? How will I accomplish what I want to achieve? How will I measure my progress?

My Answer:_____

_____

When? When will I begin working on achieving this goal?

My Answer:_____

_____

Lesson Nine

DEFINING YOUR FINANCIAL FUTURE

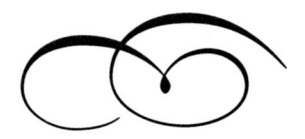

Brothers, I do not consider myself yet to have taken hold of it.
But one thing I do: Forgetting what is behind and
straining toward what is ahead, I press on toward the goal.
PHILIPPIANS 3:13-14

If you don't know where you're going, you'll end up somewhere else.
YOGI BERRA

Destiny is not a matter of chance, it is a matter of choice;
it is not a thing to be waited for, it is a thing to be achieved.
WILLIAM JENNINGS BRYAN

Success is the progressive realization of a worthy goal.
EARL NIGHTINGALE

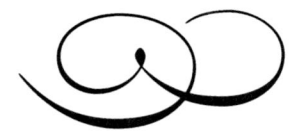

Lesson Nine

DEFINING YOUR FINANCIAL FUTURE

1. **Defining Purpose**
Write a statement of purpose – a general mission or vision statement that describes the overall intent that governs your goals, __objectives__, strategies and activities.

2. **Defining Objectives**
Determine the results you desire to achieve.

3. **Defining Goals**
Determine your goals based upon your personal values.

4. **Analyzing My Goals**
Determine the suitability of your goals based on your life circumstances.

5. **Purpose Precedes Goals**
To discover purpose in life, define objectives and achieve personal and professional goals, you must be __diligent__ in your personal commitment to the planning task at hand.

Start now by defining your purpose, your life philosophy, your objectives and then your goals.

---

6. **Dangerous Complacency**
Success requires that we __constantly__ challenge ourselves.

7. **Achievable Goals**

a. Determine direction of activity (purpose).
b. Focus on the ___*target*___ (objectives).
c. Measure at determined checkpoints (planning).
d. Establish a ___*timeline*___ for results (completion).

8. **Necessary Challenges**
   Set a course of achievement and reward for your life.

9. **Risking Another Bump**
   When we, despite the risk of experiencing some failure, strive to reach our full ___*potential*___, we will reach it and inspire others to do the same.

10. **Why Goals Are Not Set**
    a. Goals are never set by some because of the fear of failure.
    b. Many do not set goals because of lack of ___*determination*___ to stay with the task until it becomes a reality.
    c. Others are professional procrastinators.

11. **Take the Procrastinator Test.**
    Answer each question with one of the responses on the following continuum: never (1 point); some times (2); half the time (3); most of the time (4); always (5).
    How often do I...?
    a. Put off doing something I have to get done?
    b. Wait to move until someone forces or strongly encourages me to do something?
    c. Look for reasons (or excuses) not to do something I should do?
    d. Fail to complete projects I've started?
    e. Allow myself pleasant indulgences (over-sleeping, over-eating, skipping responsibilities, etc.)?
    f. Find that I've run out of time to complete a project properly because I didn't start soon enough?
    g. Allow obstacles and difficulties to prevent me from completing a project?

Add up your score and see how you rate!

7-9	If you're so conscientious, why aren't you working?
10-18	You're starting to sound truthful.
19-25	With a little practice, you might never get anything done.
26-34	How did you get around to finishing this test?
35	You're hopeless!

12. The Caterpillar Complex
Be careful not to define your goals on the aimless direction of others.

13. A Worthwhile Goal
Goal setting should bring out the best in a person, allowing him to stretch.

14. Effective Goals that Last
Goals that endure are: visualized, achievable, written, measurable, manageable, reviewed, reviewed, deadline-oriented, and rewarded.

15. Achieving Improvement
Clarity of purpose and direction is instrumental to improvement.

The planning process is no better than the goal, the goal is no better than the objective, and the objective is no better than the purpose or reason for existing.

---

16. Having Clear Goals
    a. Focuses the Mind
    b. Channels Energy
    c. Gives _**structure**_ to Your Life
    d. Requires Commitment to Accomplish Specific Things
    e. Provides Motivation

Biblical Principles for Financial Success   Teacher Workbook

   f. Makes Reaching Goals __*Habit*__ Forming
   g. Generates New Goal Setting When Results Are Achieved

17. **Focusing on Your Financial Goals**
    a. Short-Term Financial Goals
    b. Intermediate __*Financial*__ Goals
    c. Long-Range Financial Goals
    d. The Hierarchy of Goals

18. **Setting Financial Goals**
    a. It gives you control.
    b. It points you in the __*right*__ direction.
    c. It helps you know yourself.
    d. It keeps you on track.
    e. It helps you to __*build*__ financial assets.
    f. It helps you prepare for retirement.
    g. It helps with educational expenses.
    h. It __*prepares*__ you for the unexpected.
    i. It improves family communication.

19. **Steps to Goal Setting**
    a. Write down your financial goals.
    b. Give yourself a deadline.
    c. Set your __*standards*__ high.
    d. Get realistic, obtainable goals.
    e. Be __*detailed*__ and specific.
    f. Be flexible.
    g. Begin with the first step.

20. **Overview of Goals**

21. **The Planning Process**

a. Though it may seem intimidating or overwhelming, once you start __planning__ ahead and building a solid financial strategy for success, it becomes easier.

b. Planning is knowing where you are today, outlining the steps it will take to reach your financial goals, __developing__ a sound plan and continuing to follow the pattern you outlined until your goals are met.

22. Why Plan?
a. To Achieve Your Financial Goals
b. To Put Your __Ideas__ to Work
c. To Be Prepared
d. To Cope with Change
e. To Be in Control
f. To Decide What You Want to Do with Your Money
g. To Decide How Your Money Should __Work__ for You

23. Take Time to Plan
Good planning is essential to meeting financial goals.

24. Planning Checklist
a. Set specific __measurements__ of progress.
b. Outline procedures.
c. Assign activities.

25. Quality Planning
a. Importance
b. Constructing the Plan
c. Following the Plan
d. Evaluating the Plan
e. Revising and __updating__ the Plan

Notes

Lesson 9: Defining Your Financial Future

STUDENT RESPONSE

IMPROVEMENT ACTION PLAN

What I need to change:_____

What? I define my goal as this achievable result. What will be my final outcome?

My Answer:_____

_____

Why? This is why I need to accomplish my goal.

My Answer:_____

_____

Who? Who will be involved in making me successful?

My Answer:_____

_____

Where? Where will I get started? In what area will I begin?

My Answer:_____

_____

How? How will I accomplish what I want to achieve? How will I measure my progress?

My Answer:_____

_____

When? When will I begin working on achieving this goal?

My Answer:_____

_____

Notes

Module 4

Spending Management

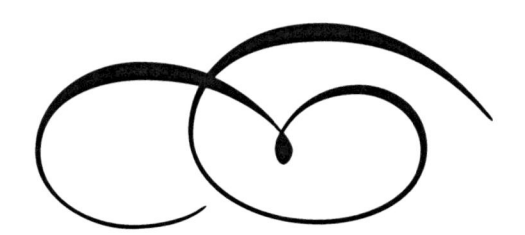

Lesson Ten

MANAGING YOUR CASH FLOW

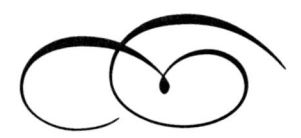

When that year was over, they came to him the following year and said, "We cannot hide from our lord the fact that since our money is gone and our livestock belongs to you, there is nothing left for our lord except our bodies and our land.
GENESIS 47:18

Ultimately, it's not what you earn that gives you financial security, but what you save.

It is not what you'd do with a million
If riches should e'er be your lot.
But what you are doing at present
With the dollar and a quarter you've got.
R.G. LeTourneau

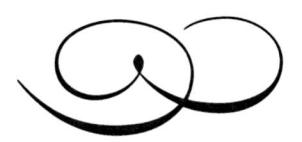

Lesson Ten

MANAGING YOUR CASH FLOW

1. **Managing Cash Flow by Finding Missing Money**
   a. A system to _**account**_ for spending and cash flow is necessary.
   b. Check stubs, receipts and charge account statements paint the big picture, but pocket money must also be accounted for.
   c. It's easy to stumble, make wrong choices and let go of personal _**discipline**_, but you can get back on track.

2. **Managing Cash Flow by Recording Spending**
   a. Getting an Easy Start
      Record daily _**expenses**_ in a pocket-sized journal.
   b. Setting up Expense Categories
      i. Determine narrow expense categories for the most detailed _**picture**_ of monthly spending.
      ii. Enter these into a simple ledger pad ruled with one wide column and at least six columns on the right for entering figures.
      iii. Recognize which expenses are _**fixed**_ and which are variable.
      iv. Record savings, preferably 10% or more of your income, as a fixed expense that you "pay yourself" monthly.
      v. Record fixed expenses directly in the ledger and variable expenses once a month (as taken from the _**daily**_ journal).
      vi. Label each page of the journal with the categories.
   c. Keeping Good Spending Records
      Record each day's expenses in the right category every evening.
   d. Totaling the Spending
   i. Total the specific _**categories**_ and record your journal each month and each total in the ledger.

Biblical Principles for Financial Success   Teacher Workbook

      ii. When the daily journal is properly kept, monthly totaling should take only a half-hour.
      iii. If your expenses exceeded your income, consider what __discretionary__ spending you could cut down on the next month.
   e. Staying with the Process
      Repeat the process for three to six months.
   f. Record-Keeping Basics
      i. Income
      ii. Salary
      iii. Accuracy
      iv. Continuity
   g. Tracking the Little Stuff
      i. Keeping track of small change, turns casual __spending__ into a conscious, ordered process by linking the act of spending money with the act of recording the expense.
      ii. After three to six months of recording, your ledger page becomes a __mathematical__ model of your finances over time.
      iii. Consider using Excel spreadsheets or investing in a money management program for your computer.
      iv. As you develop this system, you will find yourself setting goals and establishing priorities, the necessary __framework__ for a realistic personal financial plan.

3. **Managing Cash Flow by Right Spending**
   a. Tithe and Savings First
   b. Living Expenses Next
   c. Debt Reduction
   d. Wants Last

4. **Managing Cash Flow by Watching the Cash**
   Accounting and budgeting will assist you in managing your financial picture.

STUDENT RESPONSE
IMPROVEMENT ACTION PLAN

What I need to change:_____

What? I define my goal as this achievable result. What will be my final outcome?

My Answer:_____

_____

Why? This is why I need to accomplish my goal.

My Answer:_____

_____

Who? Who will be involved in making me successful?

My Answer:_____

_____

Where? Where will I get started? In what area will I begin?

My Answer:_____

_____

How? How will I accomplish what I want to achieve? How will I measure my progress?

My Answer:_____

_____

When? When will I begin working on achieving this goal?

My Answer:_____

_____

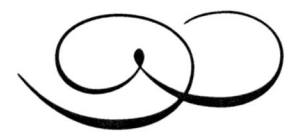

Lesson Eleven

Financial Benefits of Budgeting

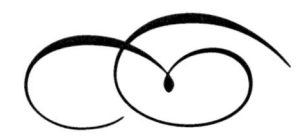

Suppose one of you wants to build a tower.
Will he not first sit down and estimate the cost
to see if he has enough money to complete it?
Luke 14:28

Persistence is stubbornness with a purpose.
Richard DeVos, Co-founder, Amway

Lesson Eleven

FINANCIAL BENEFITS OF BUDGETING

1. **Introduction**
   a. Families who have everything under control and who are financially __free__ still need a budget.
   b. When we spend more than we earn, the lack of money can contribute to much unhappiness.
   c. Properly managed money can __enhance__ family relationships.
   d. Preparation of a meaningful budget depends on keeping accurate records.

Budgets aren't records of expenses, they are forecasts of expenses.

---

2. **Principles**
   - Budgeting is a __tool__ for managing money.
   - Budgeting stops unnecessary spending.
   - Budgeting helps you break bad habits.
   - Budgeting __opens__ the door to financial security.
   - Budgeting gives your family a spending plan.
   - Budgeting will help you get in shape financially.
   - Budgeting helps you __keep__ the money you earn.
   - Budgeting will help you become debt-free.
   - Budgeting will free you, not confine you.

Biblical Principles for Financial Success   Teacher Workbook

"The mind of man plans his way, but the Lord directs his steps." (Proverbs 16:9)

- Budgeting is scriptural.

"Know well the condition of your flocks, and pay attention to your herds." (Proverbs 27:23)

- Budgeting is a ___team___ effort.
- Budgeting will make you disciplined.
- A budget for family spending gives order to family money.
- Budgeting gives you financial ___balance___ and order.
- A budget for family spending provides a blueprint for reaching goals.
- A budget systematizes one's money affairs and aids in accomplishing goals.
- A budget begins with a statement of family income.
- A budget informs you of the fixed ___expenses___ to which the family is commited.
- A budget provides for the necessary variable expenses.
- A budget will help you with the big-ticket purchases.
- Budgeting helps you prepare in advance.
- Budgeting helps you attain special ___goals___.
- Budgeting gives you another chance.
- Budgeting is tailor-made for your family.
- Budgeting makes your money do what you want it to.
    i) All goals must be based ___realistically___ on your projected budget.
    ii) Provide for the basics first, then the comforts, and finally the luxuries.
    iii) Set up a plan for paying off debts already accumulated.
    iv) Plan for savings, no matter how small. Increase your savings allocation as your old debts are reduced.
    v) Control your spending according to your budget.
    vi) Never give in to ___temptations___ to depart from the budget.
    vii) If you stumble, don't give up; regroup and get on task again.
- Budgeting is an effective management tool.

Lesson 11: Financial Benefits of Budgeting

- Budgeting gives you a financial blueprint.
- Budgeting allows you to know what is going on.
- Budgeting __gives__ you financial control.
- Budgeting provides organization.
- Budgeting encourages communication.
- A budget allows you to take __advantage__ of opportunities.
- Budgeting offers you extra time.
- Budgeting brings you extra money.

NOTES

Lesson 11: Financial Benefits of Budgeting

STUDENT RESPONSE
IMPROVEMENT ACTION PLAN

What I need to change:_____

What? I define my goal as this achievable result. What will be my final outcome?

My Answer:_____

_____

Why? This is why I need to accomplish my goal.

My Answer:_____

_____

Who? Who will be involved in making me successful?

My Answer:_____

_____

Where? Where will I get started? In what area will I begin?

My Answer:_____

_____

How? How will I accomplish what I want to achieve? How will I measure my progress?

My Answer:_____

_____

When? When will I begin working on achieving this goal?

My Answer:_____

_____

Lesson Twelve

DESIGNING THE PERFECT BUDGET

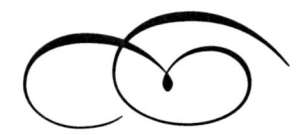

Make it your ambition to lead a quiet life,
to mind your own business and to work with your hands,
just as we told you, so that your daily life may win the
respect of outsiders and so that you will not be dependent on anybody.
I THESSALONIANS 4:11-12

Never spend your money before you have it.
THOMAS JEFFERSON

Lesson Twelve

DESIGNING THE PERFECT BUDGET

1. **First Steps to Wealth**
   a. Take control of your income and outgo.
   b. Be in __*control*__ of your financial future.

2. **How Do I Get Started?**
   a. First, categorize and list all regular expenses.
   b. Next, fill in the blanks on the spreadsheet.
   c. Try to better __*analyze*__ your expenses, but don't forget to ask God for guidance.

   Jeremiah 17:7, 8; James 4:10

A budget is a powerful method of gaining control, planning, communicating, and fulfilling your dreams.

---

3. **Making Your Budget Work**
   Consider setting up a budget __*worksheet*__ with your expense categories in the left column and fifteen additional columns.
   Column 1 – amount budgeted per month per category
   Columns 2-13 – January through December actual costs
   Column 14 – total annual costs
   Column 15 – average monthly costs

Biblical Principles for Financial Success   Teacher Workbook

4. **Some Budgeting Tips**
   a. Be patient.
   b. Invest or ___*save*___ any windfall income.
   c. If you have a quarterly, semiannual or annual payment, save that amount each month so it doesn't throw off your budget.
   d. Don't forget to pay yourself. Save something each month that can go toward an investment.
   e. Don't try to track every penny – it will drive you and everyone else nuts.
   f. Make ___*impulse*___ buying difficult – leave your checkbook and credit cards at home.
   g. Set aside some fun money for each family member.
   h. Budget for fun (vacation, toy).
   i. Don't over-categorize (too many expense categories).
   j. Don't use her paycheck for certain things and his for others.
   k. Use an ___*interest bearing*___ checking account.
   l. Record savings as an expense item.
   m. Create an "expense" item to pay off credit-card balances.
   n. Pay off cards with the highest interest rate first.
   o. Don't use credit cards again until the ___*balance*___ is paid off.
   p. Once a loan is paid off, keep paying the amount to yourself (make a vacation fund or car fund).
   q. Set aside money monthly for bills due quarterly, semi-annually, or yearly.
   r. Reconcile your ___*budget*___ at least once a month when reconciling your checking statement.
   s. Make sure to mark your last reconcile point in your budget.
   t. Just identifying your expenses is extremely valuable.

5. **How to Organize Your Monthly, Quarterly and Annual Bills**
   a. Pay your bills ___*promptly*___ to avoid late fees.
   b. Follow basic steps to keep you from procrastination.
   c. Always put your bills in a specific place when they arrive.
   d. Set aside ___*two*___ times a month, two weeks apart, to pay bills.

e. Ask the companies that bill you to revise your payment due dates to correspond with one of these two times.
f. Mark bill-paying dates on your calendar and pay on schedule.
g. Pay with checks or money orders and __record__ the check number, date, and amount you paid on the payment receipt.
h. File payment receipts and keep them for up to seven years.
i. Place payment envelopes next to your car or house keys so you __remember__ to mail them immediately.
j. Don't forget to take them all the way to the mailbox!
k. Check due dates for bills as soon as they arrive in the mail, as this can sometimes change.

6. **Why Budgets Fail**
    a. Unrealistic Goals
    b. Quitting Too Soon
    c. Misunderstanding What a __Budget__ Really Is
    d. Family Or Spousal Strife
    e. Going to Extremes
    f. The "More-Money-In, More-Money-Out" Syndrome
    g. Thinking That a Little __Debt__ Won't Hurt
    h. Using Automatic Checking Account Overdrafts
    i. Misuse of Automatic Teller Machines (ATM)
    j. Refusing to Balance Your Checkbook
    k. The Common Feeling of Simple Discouragement
    l. Wrong __Thinking__: "I Don't Have Enough Money to Budget!"
    m. Not Teaching Your Children

    "Instruct them to do good, to be rich in good works, to be generous and ready to share, storing up for themselves the treasure of a good foundation for the future, so that they may take hold of that which is life indeed." (I Timothy 6:18-19)

NOTES

STUDENT RESPONSE

IMPROVEMENT ACTION PLAN

What I need to change:_____

What? I define my goal as this achievable result. What will be my final outcome?

My Answer:_____

_____

Why? This is why I need to accomplish my goal.

My Answer:_____

_____

Who? Who will be involved in making me successful?

My Answer:_____

_____

Where? Where will I get started? In what area will I begin?

My Answer:_____

_____

How? How will I accomplish what I want to achieve? How will I measure my progress?

My Answer:_____

_____

When? When will I begin working on achieving this goal?

My Answer:_____

_____

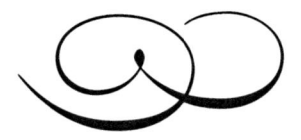

Lesson Thirteen

DEVELOPING THE SAVINGS HABIT

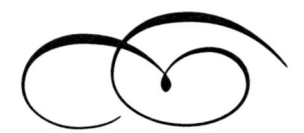

The plans of the diligent lead to profit
as surely as haste leads to poverty.
PROVERBS 21:5

Diamonds are nothing more than chunks of coal
that stuck to their job.
MALCOLM FORBES

Lesson Thirteen

DEVELOPING THE SAVINGS HABIT

1. **Strategy**
   a. First, put your money into a rainy-day fund.
   b. Save for __long range__ expenses.
   c. Save for retirement.
   d. Set up automatic payroll deduction.
   e. Set up automatic bank transfers.
   f. Invest __increases__ in salary.
   g. Invest lump sum payments like tax refunds and bonuses.

2. **You Can Begin Saving Now**
   a. Set savings goals.
   b. Pay yourself first.
   c. Throw __stumbling__ blocks in the path of spending.
   d. Save all extra money.

3. **You Can Make Your Savings Grow Faster**
   a. Money Market Funds
   b. Stock __Mutual__ Funds
   c. US Treasuries

4. **How you Can Save**
   a. Develop new habits.
   c. Don't buy on impulse.
   d. Get rid of __credit__ card debt.
   e. Use installment credit sparingly.

f. Take good care of your assets.
g. Update your homeowner's insurance policy.
h. Update your life insurance policy.
i. Start a _retirement_ fund.
j. Get the best health insurance possible.
k. Pay off your mortgage faster.
l. Use non-money resources.
m. Develop good _spending_ habits.
n. Choose quality over price.
o. Pause before purchasing and ask. . .
   i. Can I really _afford_ it?
   ii. Do I really need it?
   iii. Is it worth what I'm paying?
o. Save by _doing_ things yourself.
   i. Wash your car yourself.
   ii. Review insurance policies to avoid overlapping coverage.
   iii. Buy a used car.
   iv. Eat out for _lunch_ instead of dinner.
   v. Trade down in suits, travel arrangements, rental car size.
   vi. Look for a package when planning a trip.
   vii. Don't dispose of clothing you are tired of. Put it away for a season or two and you will _appreciate_ it again later.
   viii. Turn down the thermostat during winter and wear a sweater.
   ix. Buy holiday items after Christmas at half price and save them.
   x. Turn off the lights when you leave a room.
   xi. Jog or use public _recreation_ areas instead of paying for a gym.
   xii. Save unused gifts with the giver's name and give to someone else a year later.
   xiii. Use _free_ and low-cost offers/coupons.
   xiv. Borrow books at the library instead of buying them.
   xv. Use plastic/paper bags from the store as garbage bags.
   xvi. Return bottles and cans to the store and receive your deposit.

Lesson 13: Developing the Savings Habit

  xvii. Reuse paper clips.

  xviii. Cut your own hair and that of family members.

  xix. Trade hand-me-downs with friends and relatives

 p. Exercise ___personal___ discipline.

 q. Understand inflation.

Item Purchased Today	Cost in 20 Years (4.5% average annual inflation rate)	Cost in 20 Years (3.5% average annual inflation rate)
Coffee & Scone $7	$16.88	$13.93
Steak for 1 $20	$48.23	$39.80
A Weekend Away $500	$1,205.86	$994.89

 r. The Power of ___Compound___ Interest

 s. Begin while you're young.

 t. Learn how to invest..

Notes

Lesson 13: Developing the Savings Habit

STUDENT RESPONSE
IMPROVEMENT ACTION PLAN

What I need to change:_____

What? I define my goal as this achievable result. What will be my final outcome?

My Answer:_____

_____

Why? This is why I need to accomplish my goal.

My Answer:_____

_____

Who? Who will be involved in making me successful?

My Answer:_____

_____

Where? Where will I get started? In what area will I begin?

My Answer:_____

_____

How? How will I accomplish what I want to achieve? How will I measure my progress?

My Answer:_____

_____

When? When will I begin working on achieving this goal?

My Answer:_____

_____

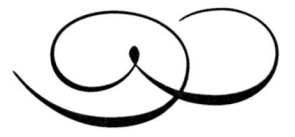

Lesson Fourteen

BORROWING AND CREDIT ISSUES

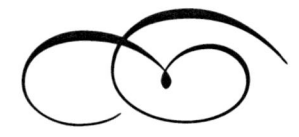

*Just as the rich rule the poor,
so the borrower is servant to the lender.*
PROVERBS 22:7 (TLB)

Lesson Fourteen

BORROWING AND CREDIT ISSUES

1. **Do You Borrow Too Quickly?**

   God wants to ____reveal____ Himself as our Provider.

   "Not that I am looking for a gift, but I am looking for what may be credited to your account. I have received full payment and even more; I am amply supplied, now that I have received from Epaphroditus the gifts you sent. They are a fragrant offering, an acceptable sacrifice, pleasing to God. And my God will meet all your needs according to his glorious riches in Christ Jesus." (Philippians 4:17-19)

   "Let the wicked forsake his way and the evil man his thoughts. Let him turn to the LORD, and He will have mercy on him, and to our God, for He will freely pardon. 'For My thoughts are not your thoughts, neither are your ways My ways,' declares the LORD. 'As the heavens are higher than the earth, so are My ways higher than your ways and My thoughts than your thoughts.'" (Isaiah 55:7-9)

   a. Getting into ____debt____ is simple.
   b. The Lifestyle of Debt
   c. Borrowing Money with the ____right____ Intentions

   "Obey the laws, then, for two reasons: first, to keep from being punished, and second, just because you know you should. Pay your taxes too, for these same two reasons. For government workers need to be paid so that they can keep on doing God's work, serving you. Pay everyone whatever he ought to have: pay your taxes and import duties gladly, obey those over you, and give honor and respect to all those to whom it is due. Pay all your debts except the debt of love for others— never finish paying that! For if you love them, you will be obeying all of God's laws, fulfilling all his requirement." (Romans 13:5-8, TLB)

"The wicked borrow and do not repay, but the righteous give generously." (Psalms 37:21)

d. Living a __Self controlled__ Lifestyle

"Now the overseer must be above reproach… temperate, self-controlled, respectable…" (I Timothy 3:2)

"Thus says the LORD, your Redeemer, the Holy One of Israel: 'I am the LORD your God, who teaches you to profit, who leads you by the way you should go." (Isaiah 48:17, NKJ)

e. The __Problem__ of Easy Credit

"Now listen, you who say, 'Today or tomorrow we will go to this or that city, spend a year there, carry on business and make money.' Why, you do not even know what will happen tomorrow. What is your life? You are a mist that appears for a little while and then vanishes. Instead, you ought to say, 'If it is the Lord's will, we will live and do this or that.'" (James 4:13-15)

f. The __Bondage__ of Debt

"The rich rule over the poor, and the borrower is servant to the lender." (Proverbs 22:7)

g. Is credit debt dangerous?
h. Secrets of __Borrowing__ Less
i. Pledge Yourself to Delayed Gratification
j. Credit Card Debt
k. Credit Card Interest
l. Warning Signs __Impending__ Financial Disaster

"The alien who lives among you will rise above you higher and higher, but you will sink lower and lower. He will lend to you, but you will not lend to him. He will be the head, but you will be the tail." (Deuteronomy 28:43-45)

m. How can I get help?

"So I say to you: Ask and it will be given to you; seek and you will find; knock and the door will be opened to you. For everyone who asks receives; he who seeks finds; and to him who knocks, the door will be opened." (Luke 11:9-10)

    n. The Importance of Being Credit-Worthy
    o. Managing Your __Credit__ Intelligently
    p. How much debt is too much?
    q. Breaking Free from the Spending Habit
    r. Credit cards are not an __extension__ of your paycheck.
    s. Paying as You Go
    t. How to Avoid Excessive Debt
    u. Owing More than Your Assets
    v. Talk with Your Creditors
    w. A __Spotless__ Credit Record

In essence, you slide into debt and have to climb out. Easy in, not so easy out.

---

2. **How Credit Reports Work**
   a. Identifying Information
   b. Credit Information
   c. Public Record Information
   d. Inquiries
   e. How is credit __information__ used?
   f. Only data is analyzed.

3. **How To Improve Your Credit Score**
   a. Close __accounts__ you're not using.
   b. Don't hit all your credit limits.
   c. Manage inquiries into your record.

d. Automate to be on time.
   e. Don't allow _delinquent_ payments.
   f. Check your credit report.
   g. Beware of mistakes.
   h. Beware of _fraudulent_ credit cleaning companies.

4. **Credit Scoring**
   a. Payment History (35%)
   b. Outstanding Debt (30%)
   c. Length of Your Credit History (15%)
   d. Types of Credit in Use (10%)
   e. Recent Inquiries (10%)
   f. The _Range_ of Scores

5. **How To Get Higher Credit Scores**
   a. Pay your bills on time.
   b. Keep credit card _balances_ low.
   c. Keep no more than one or two credit cards.
   d. Make sure your credit records are accurate.

Cultivate the mindset that you will only borrow for absolute necessities.

---

6. **Why Do I Have Credit Problems?**
   Creditors evaluate borrowers upon character, capacity, and collateral.

7. **What Is Less than Perfect Credit?**
   a. Revolving or Installment Credit (e.g. Credit Card, Car Loan)
      More than two 30-days (or one 60-days) past-due payments
   b. Housing Debt - Any past-due payments

Lesson 14: Borrowing and Credit Issues

8. **Rebuilding Credit FAQ's**
   a. How to __Rebuild__ Your Credit Rating
   b. Cleaning up Your Credit Report
   c. Obtaining a Copy of Your Credit Report
      You will need to provide the following information to the three major credit bureaus – Equifax, Trans Union and Experian:
      i. Your full name (include Jr., Sr., III, etc.)
      ii. Your birth date
      iii. Your social security number
      iv. Your spouse's name
      v. Your telephone number
      vi. Your five-year address history
   d. What should I do if I find __mistakes__ in my credit report?
   e. What can I do to rebuild my credit?

9. **Debt Consolidation**
   a. Don't Consolidate If…
      i. Your habits will not change.
      ii. The interest rate to __consolidate__ will be high.
   b. Seriously Consider Consolidating to…
      i. Stop creditor harassment.
      ii. Lower monthly payments.
      iii. Reduce interest and late fee charges.

Biblical Principles for Financial Success   Teacher Workbook

STUDENT RESPONSE

IMPROVEMENT ACTION PLAN

What I need to change:_____

What? I define my goal as this achievable result. What will be my final outcome?

My Answer:_____

_____

Why? This is why I need to accomplish my goal.

My Answer:_____

_____

Who? Who will be involved in making me successful?

My Answer:_____

_____

Where? Where will I get started? In what area will I begin?

My Answer:_____

_____

How? How will I accomplish what I want to achieve? How will I measure my progress?

My Answer:_____

_____

When? When will I begin working on achieving this goal?

My Answer:_____

_____

Module 5

Making Lifestyle Changes

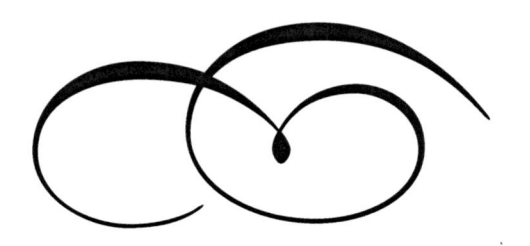

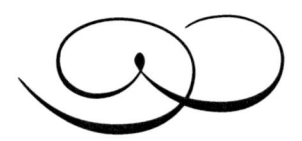

Lesson Fifteen

GETTING OUT OF DEBT

No discipline seems pleasant at the time, but painful.
Later on, however, it produces a harvest of . . .
peace for those who have been trained by it.
HEBREWS 12:11

Creditors have better memories than debtors.
BENJAMIN FRANKLIN

Lesson Fifteen

GETTING OUT OF DEBT

Perform a simple financial check-up to ensure that you are not headed for serious trouble.

1. **Actions – Not Just Good Intentions**
   By looking at your income and __expenses__ for the past month, you can roughly determine your financial health.

2. **Danger Signals of Too Much Debt**
   Debt problems can be spotted before they become serious, so take a look!

3. **Do You Have a Credit Problem?**
   Most people need to borrow at some point and a good credit rating is __essential__ for fulfilling most financial goals in life.

4. **Forming Good Habits vs. Bad Habits**
   Let your __habits__ work for you, not against you.

5. **Small Efforts Equal Huge Rewards**
   Small changes we make can have significant effects when maintained over a long period of time.

6. **A Lesson Learned**
   Accomplishing great things does not require acts of __heroism__, but only small, consistent, and determined steps toward a goal.

7. **A Simple Guide to Climbing Out of Debt**

8. **Determine Not to Overspend**

Biblical Principles for Financial Success   Teacher Workbook

This chart shows the difference made by a ___small___ change like making your own lunch one extra day a week.

Number of Days Eating Out for Lunch	Number of Days Making Your Lunch	Total Lunch Expense	Annual Lunch Expense
5 days per week	0 days per week	$35	$1,750
4 days per week	1 day per week	$29	$1,450
3 days per week	2 days per week	$23	$1,150
2 days per week	3 days per week	$17	$850
1 day per week	4 days per week	$11	$550
0 days per week	5 days per week	$5	$250

9. **Avoid Adding New Debts**
   Cut up credit cards upon which you have no ___balance___ and close the accounts by calling your creditors.

10. **Develop a Debt-Management Plan**
    (The following steps are adapted from *Getting out of Debt, How Others Can Help You Get out of Debt* and the Mississippi and Virginia Cooperative Extension.)
    a. Find out how much you ___owe___ and to whom.
    b. Decide how much you can pay back and when.
    c. Set up a plan for paying back your debts.
    d. Discuss your ___plan___ with your creditors.
    e. Control spending by sticking with your debt-payment plan until debts are repaid.

11. **Paying Back Your Debts**
    Debt payment can be done in several ways.
    a. Pay each creditor equal amounts.

Lesson 15: Getting Out of Debt

Debt	Amount Owed	Amount Required	Amount Able to Pay
Auto Loan	$1,145.39	$180	$60
Visa	680.30	35	60
Debt 1	525.00	170	60
Debt 2	755.00	190	60
Debt 3	275.00	25	60
	$3,380.69	**$600**	**$300**

b. Pay a larger portion to whom you owe the most and a smaller portion to whom you owe the least.

Debt	Amount Owed	Percent of Total	Amount Required	Amount Able to Pay
Auto Loan	$1,145.39	34%	$180	$102
Visa	680.30	20%	35	60
Debt 1	525.00	16%	170	48
Debt 2	755.00	22%	190	66
Debt 3	275.00	8%	25	24
	$3,380.69	**100%**	**$600**	**$300**

c. Figure what percent of the required amount you can afford to pay and pay that percentage to each creditor.

Debt	Amount Owed	Amount Required	Amount Able to Pay
Auto Loan	$1,145.39	$180 (x .50)	$90.00
Visa	680.30	35 (x .50)	17.50
Debt 1	525.00	170 (x .50)	85.00
Debt 2	755.00	190 (x .50)	95.00
Debt 3	275.00	25 (x .50)	12.50
	$3,380.69	**$600**	**$300**

12. Prioritizing Your Debt
When sufficient funds are not available to pay amounts required, consider __*prioritizing*__: i.e. mortgage first, credit cards second...

13. Communicate with Creditors
Creditors are __*impressed*__ when you come up with a plan and even more so when you follow it – get them to agree with your plan.

14. Set a Financial Goal
Set a realistic goal for when you will be debt-free, i.e. 3 years.

15. Create a Spending Plan
   a. Determine your __*net*__ worth.
   b. Track your cash flow.
   c. Evaluate your monthly income sources.
   d. Record your __*monthly*__ expenses.
   e. Keep a written account of your progress.
   f. List all you owe first.
   g. Create a __*payoff*__ plan.
   h. Assess the damage.
   i. Pay the most expensive loan first.
   j. Transfer your debts to a low-interest-rate credit card.
   k. Cut up the high-rate cards you've paid off so you won't use them again.
   l. Have a yard sale.
   m. Keep a record of your __*current*__ living expenses for a month.
   n. Consider selling assets.
   o. Increase your family income.
   p. Borrow money as a last resort.

16. Determine & Reduce Your Time Goal
Because of compound interest, cutting the time you pay off a debt in half does not mean doubling the monthly payment, but rather slightly raising it.

Lesson 15: Getting Out of Debt

17. **Stay Focused on the Plan and Be Persistent.**

18. **Becoming Debt-Free**
    It is possible for most ___families___ to get out of debt within four years.

19. **Simple – But Not Easy**
    When you encounter difficulties, don't run away from your creditors, ___communicate___ with them. Consumer credit counseling organizations also provide a helpful third party.

20. **Your Decision to Change**
    Becoming debt-free can only happen if you are ___totally___ committed.

21. **Debt-Free Is Only the Beginning**

    > **Like boot camp, becoming debt–free is not the end; rather, it's the beginning of a whole new adventure.**

22. **The Picture of No Debt**
    The debt-free lifestyle looks like this.
    a. You spend less than you earn.
    b. You give.
    c. You save.
    d. You invest ___confidently___ and consistently.
    e. Your financial decisions are purposeful.
    f. You turn away from impulsive behavior.
    g. You shun unsecured debt.
    h. You borrow cautiously.
    i. You ___anticipate___ the unexpected.
    j. You scrutinize your purchases.
    k. You reach for your goals by following a ___specific___ plan.

23. Handling Debt: The Courtroom

Handling debt by turning to the legal system is often costly and can involve serious financial consequences in the future.

24. Chapter 7 Bankruptcy

Filing bankruptcy allows one to be rid of most debt, but it also allows the court to liquidate their assets and pay off as much of the debt as possible.

25. Chapter 13 Wage-Earner's Plan

One can file Chapter 13 to __repay__ debts with the help of a court-ordered trustee who will garnish a percentage of wages earned to pay off debts over a period of time and help the filer manage their money.

26. Reward Yourself!

When you have come to the point of being debt-free, don't be afraid to treat yourself to an inexpensive __reward__. Just don't forget that after debt-recovery, the race to debt-prevention is on!

Lesson 15: Getting Out of Debt

STUDENT RESPONSE
IMPROVEMENT ACTION PLAN

What I need to change:_____

What? I define my goal as this achievable result. What will be my final outcome?

My Answer:_____

_____

Why? This is why I need to accomplish my goal.

My Answer:_____

_____

Who? Who will be involved in making me successful?

My Answer:_____

_____

Where? Where will I get started? In what area will I begin?

My Answer:_____

_____

How? How will I accomplish what I want to achieve? How will I measure my progress?

My Answer:_____

_____

When? When will I begin working on achieving this goal?

My Answer:_____

_____

Lesson Sixteen

Making Lifestyle Changes

By what a man is overcome, by this he is enslaved.
II Peter 2:19

Your servant . . . did this to change the present situation. . . .
Ii Samuel 14:20

The Plans of the diligent lead surely to advantage,
but everyone who is hasty comes surely to poverty.
Proverbs 21:5

If you can't feed a hundred people, then feed just one.
Mother Teresa

It's not what you make; it's what you spend.

Getting out of debt is an attitude before it is an action.

Lesson Sixteen

Making Lifestyle Changes

1. **Lifestyle Change Means Doing without the Non-Essentials**

2. **Lifestyle Change Means Paying with Cash**

3. **Lifestyle Change Means Committing to Godly Principles**

   "Blessings on all who reverence and trust the Lord— on all who obey Him! Their reward shall be prosperity and happiness." (Psalm 128:1,2)

   a. You must never keep it all.
   b. You must never _spend_ it all.
   c. God is your source.
   d. What you _receive_ is what you deserve.

4. **Lifestyle Change Means Learning Timely Principles**

5. **Lifestyle Change Means Decreasing Your Expenses**

   If Your Spending Is Out of Control…
   - As you pay off smaller debts, don't pay less each month on your overall debt, put that money towards another bill.
   - Ask for help and seek _advice_ about your situation.
   - Assess the damage.
   - Avoid _cosigning_ or guaranteeing a loan for someone.
   - Avoid further credit.
   - Avoid joint obligations with people who have _questionable_ spending habits.
   - Avoid large rent or house payments.

- Avoid __unnecessary__ items (even if they're on sale).
- Barter your skills for someone else's skills.
- Be aware of the difference between wants and needs.
- Be aware of your spending habits.
- Be patient.

There are only five things you can do with money: give it, save it, invest it, lend it, and spend it.

- Bring your lunch to work.
- Buy creative gifts as opposed to expensive gifts.
- Buy used items rather than new.
- Charge items only if you can __afford__ to pay for them now.
- Clip coupons and use them.
- Create a realistic budget and stick to it.
- Create a __spending__ plan.
- Credit Cards
    i. Pay more than the minimum monthly payment.
    ii. Never use them to buy unbudgeted items.
    iii. Pay off the balance in full each month.
    iv. If you can't pay the whole monthly balance, destroy it!
    v. Cut up cards for gas or department stores.
    vi. Cut up high-rate cards you've paid off.
- Cut housing costs.
- Cut out __expensive__ entertainment.
- Cut your cost of transportation.
- Deposit money in a __savings__ account regularly and leave it there.

- Determine your net worth.
- Develop a balanced budget that allows creditors to receive as much as possible.
- Develop a strategy.
- Do your own chores and repairs.
- Don't be so quick to pay down your mortgage.
- Don't expect instant miracles.
- Don't go broke on "good buys".

"*By what a man is overcome, by this he is enslaved.*" (II Peter 2:19)

- Don't make __high risk__ investments.
- Drive your car an extra year or two before getting a new one.
- Eat oatmeal – it's healthy and filling.
- Eat out less and at home more.
- Eating in: use or freeze everything you buy.
- Drink __water__ instead of soda.
- Enjoy the city parks.
- Evaluate your monthly income sources.
- Expect the unexpected.
- Fast food: don't order value meals.
- Find __alternatives__ to spending money.

If you don't borrow money, you can't get into debt.

- For extra income, peddle your skills.
- Forget about buying now, paying later.
- Get at least three prices for the same item from different sources.
- Get in shape: ride your bicycle to work.

- Get ___medical___ insurance.
- Get the most for your money.
- Gifts: buy them ahead of time and keep extras to avoid costly last-minute shopping.
- Give to ___yourself___ first by saving.
- Go shopping with a list and buy only those items.
- Grow your own garden.
- Improve your gas mileage.
- Impulse ___buying___ is a form of the get-rich-quick mentality.

  "The plans of the diligent lead surely to advantage, but everyone who is hasty comes surely to poverty." (Proverbs 21:5)

- Increase your insurance ___deductibles___ to lower your monthly payment.
- Inform your kids and spouse of financial plans.
- Keep a "get rid of it" box and empty it twice annually.
- Keep a ___spending___ record and a spending plan.
- Listen carefully.
- Live within your means.
- Look around for ___better___ insurance rates.
- Maintain a one-item wish list and compare prices.
- Maintain an ___emergency___ cash fund.
- Make a plan to pay off your debts.
- Make a resolution that you will NOT overspend ever again.
- Make long-distance calls only if ___necessary___ and at off-peak times.
- Make only one trip to the grocery store each week.
- Make ___plans___ for life after debt.
- Make your own coffee.
- Make your own gifts.
- Minimize your debt.
- Most debt is bad.

Lesson 16: Making Lifestyles Changes

- Move in with your parents (but only if you are single).
- Never __borrow__ to buy depreciating items.
- Never buy anything unless you have budgeted for it.
- Only borrow for a home or college (or a car with zero percent financing).
- Pare down your __grocery__ bill — eat rice and beans.
- Pay only with cash (but save your receipts).
- Pay off the most expensive loan first.
- Pay yourself by saving after you have tithed.
- Plan for the future.
- Practice __utility__ control.

Debt is like cancer. It is not life-threatening at first when it involves only a cell or two, but it grows from there and then it takes over.

- Retail Stores: Make an offer on floor models.
- Ride public transportation.
- Save all extra money.
- Save on supplies.
- Seek __professional__ help to work your way out of debt.
- Sell the new vehicle and settle for good used reliable transportation.
- Shop at thrift clothing stores.
- Start retiring the debt now.
- Stay away from convenience stores.
- Stay healthy.
- Stay home.
- Stay out of malls.

- Stop _incurring_ debt.
- Stop spending!
- Subtract credit card purchases in your _checkbook_ register.
- Take advantage of free programs.
- There are no magic rules that solve financial troubles.
- Track your progress.
- Transfer your debts to a low-interest rate credit card.
- Try the Consumer Credit Counseling Service.
- Turn down the thermostat or air conditioning.
- Use _coupons_, rebates and special promotions.
- Vacations: try a home exchange.
- Visit your local library.
- Wait at least _ten_ days to buy non-budgeted items.
- Wait _six_ months and think it through before you purchase a "must have" item.
- When you pay off a car loan, keep investing that payment in mutual funds.
- You are never going to win the lottery so stop wasting your money.

Lesson 16: Making Lifestyles Changes

STUDENT RESPONSE

IMPROVEMENT ACTION PLAN

What I need to change:_____

What? I define my goal as this achievable result. What will be my final outcome?

My Answer:_____

_____

Why? This is why I need to accomplish my goal.

My Answer:_____

_____

Who? Who will be involved in making me successful?

My Answer:_____

_____

Where? Where will I get started? In what area will I begin?

My Answer:_____

_____

How? How will I accomplish what I want to achieve? How will I measure my progress?

My Answer:_____

_____

When? When will I begin working on achieving this goal?

My Answer:_____

_____

Lesson Seventeen

Areas of Financial Vulnerability

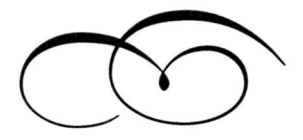

By wisdom, a house is built and
through understanding, it is established.
PROVERBS 24:3

If something seems too good to be true, it probably is.

A bank is a place where they lend you an umbrella in fair weather
and ask for it back when it begins to rain.
ROBERT FROST

When wealth is lost, nothing is lost;
when health is lost, something is lost;
when character is lost, all is lost.
BILLY GRAHAM

Lesson Seventeen

AREAS OF FINANCIAL VULNERABILITY

1. **The Vulnerability in Co-Signing**
   a. You are ___*borrowing*___ the money.
   b. You are loaning the money.
   c. You are hoping your friend or relative will pay back the loan.

> **Ask questions, check the answers and consider all the facts before making that purchase or investing those hard–earned dollars.**

2. **The Vulnerability of Credit Scams**
   Strategies to ___*ensure*___ that you are the only one using your credit cards:
   a. Don't give your social security number to anyone except a brokerage, bank or employer.
   b. Destroy documents with ___*personal*___ information before you throw them out.
   c. Demand that your credit card company stop selling your personal information (and don't give it away yourself by filling out surveys or sweepstakes entries).
   d. Contact the three credit bureaus and request that they put a "___*fraud*___ alert" on your file.

3. **The Vulnerability of Get-Rich Schemes**
   a. Extended Warranties
   b. Credit Checks

Biblical Principles for Financial Success   Teacher Workbook

    c. Debt Consolidation
    d. Too _____*Good*_____ to Be True
    e. Other Money Pits

Lesson 17: Areas of Financial Vulnerability

STUDENT RESPONSE

IMPROVEMENT ACTION PLAN

What I need to change:_____

What? I define my goal as this achievable result. What will be my final outcome?

My Answer:_____

_____

Why? This is why I need to accomplish my goal.

My Answer:_____

_____

Who? Who will be involved in making me successful?

My Answer:_____

_____

Where? Where will I get started? In what area will I begin?

My Answer:_____

_____

How? How will I accomplish what I want to achieve? How will I measure my progress?

My Answer:_____

_____

When? When will I begin working on achieving this goal?

My Answer:_____

_____

Notes

Module 6

Investing with a Vision

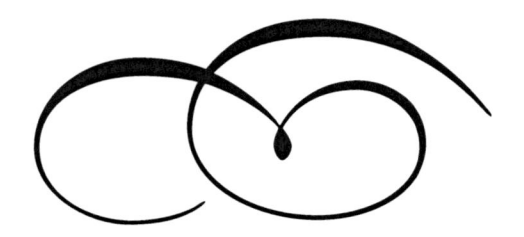

Lesson Eighteen

INVESTING FOR YOUR FUTURE

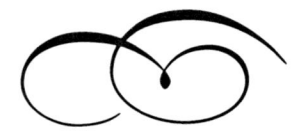

He who works his land will have abundant food,
but he who chases fantasies lacks judgment.
PROVERBS 12:11

Steady plodding brings prosperity;
hasty speculation brings poverty.
PROVERBS 21:5 (TLB)

Our callings are not simply secular means of making money or a living,
but are God's means of utilizing our gifts and interests to His glory.
A PARAPHRASE OF MARTIN LUTHER

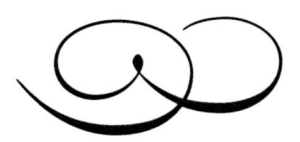

Lesson Eighteen

Investing for your Future

1. **Be Informed about Your Investment Risk**
   a. Liquidity Risk
   b. Inflation Risk
   c. Economic Risk
   d. Interest Rate Risk
   e. Market Risk
   f. Company Risk
   g. Specific Risk

2. **Know How to Minimize Your Investment Risk**
   a. Diversification across Types of Securities
   b. Diversification across ___Time___ Horizons
   c. Diversification across Industries
   d. Diversification among Different Companies

3. **Steps to Investing Disaster**
   a. The Foolishness of Failing to Set Goals
   b. The Foolishness of Giving up All Decisions to an Advisor
   c. The Foolishness of Failing to Find a Sensible Investment Strategy
   d. The Foolishness of Failing to Understand Risk and ___Diversify___ Adequately
   e. The Foolishness of Trying to Time the Stock Market
   f. The ___Foolishness___ of Driving Your Investment Strategy with Taxes

   Divide the tax-exempt yield you are considering (i.e. 7 percent) by 1 less your tax bracket. (i.e. If you fall into the 28% federal tax bracket, this number would be 1 - 0.28 = 0.72.) You would need to earn more than this number (i.e.

7 divided by 0.72 = 9.72 %) on a taxable investment to beat the return on a tax-exempt investment.

    g. The Foolishness of Aggressively Seeking the _____Highest_____ Yield
    h. The Foolishness of Relying on Past Performance only for Investment Choices
    i. The Foolishness of Underestimating the Effect of Commissions
    j. The Foolishness of Failure to Keep _____Accurate_____ Tax Records
    k. The Foolishness of Not Setting Aside Adequate Cash for Emergencies
    l. The Foolishness of Underestimating Your Retirement Obligations

    Plan to live until you are 90 and recognize that even moderate inflation of 5% annually can make your $1000 a month only worth what $277 is today.

    m. The Foolishness of Sweating the _____Small_____ Stuff

    If you are worried that another bank offers a quarter of an interest point more than yours does, don't be – you would only earn $2.50 annually per $1000 (upon which you must still pay taxes).

4. **Steps to Investing Success**
    a. Establish investment objectives and _____stick_____ with them.
    b. Invest for the long term.
    c. Stay invested.

    Generally, your money will double in the number of years equaled by the assumed interest rate divided into 72. (i.e. An investment at 7.5 percent will double in nine and a half years.)

    d. Practice dollar-cost averaging.

    By investing the same amount of money at _____regular_____ intervals, you will purchase fewer shares at high prices and more shares at lower prices, thus avoiding the guesswork involved in timing market ups and downs.

    e. How does dollar-cost averaging work?

f. An Old Proverb

An old proverb says, "Steady plodding brings prosperity; hasty speculation brings poverty." (Proverbs 21:5, TLB)

5. **Principles of Investing in Mutual Funds**
   a. The Principle of Seeking Out ___Low cost___ Funds
      i. Avoid stock funds with annual expenses that total more than 1.5% of the invested assets.
      ii. With international funds, this should be 2% or less.
      iii. With bond funds, insist on expenses below 1%.
   b. The Principle of Dollar-Cost Averaging
   c. The Principle of Building a ___Well balanced___ and Diversified Portfolio
   d. The Principle of Understanding Market Indexes
      i. S&P Composite Index
      ii. Dow Jones Industrial Average
      iii. NYSE Composite Index
      iv. Amex Market Value Index
      v. NASDAQ Composite Index
      vi. Russell 1000, 2000, 3000
      vii. Wilshire 5000
      viii. S&P Midcap 400

6. **Online Educational Courses**
   - Schwab.com
   - kiplinger.com
   - finance.yahoo.com
   - smartmoney.com
   - businessweek.com
   - money.cnn.com
   - fortune.com

Biblical Principles for Financial Success   Teacher Workbook

- bloomberg.com
- investing.rutgers.edu
- morningstar.com
- quicken.com
- siebertnet.com
- moneycentral.msn.com
- flagship.vanguard.com
- fidelity.com
- standardandpoors.com

7. **Alternatives for Your Investment Consideration**
   a. Investment in Cash
   b. Investment in Bonds
   c. Investment in __Treasury__ Securities
   d. Treasury Notes And Bonds
   e. Zero Coupon Bonds
   f. Investment in Agency Securities
   g. Investment in Corporate Bonds
   h. Investment in __Municipal__ Bonds
   i. Investment in Common Stocks
   j. Investment in Money Market Funds
   k. Investment in Bond Mutual Funds
      i. U.S. Government Bond Funds
      ii. Mortgage-Backed __Securities__ Funds
      iii. Corporate Bond Funds
      iv. Municipal Bond Funds
      v. Current income
      vi. Diversification
      vii. Stability
      viii. Professional management
      ix. Liquidity

x. Convenience
xi. Tax consequences
xii. Income fluctuation
l. Investment in ___Stock___ Mutual Funds
  i. Growth Funds
  ii. Value Funds
  iii. Blend Funds
  iv. Small-Cap
  v. Mid-Cap
  vi. Large-Cap
m. Investment in Balanced Mutual Funds

The key to investing: Diversify.

---

8. **Portfolio Strategy**
   a. Risk Level I: ___Preservation___ of Capital
      i. 20% Money Market Funds
      ii. 20% High Quality Bonds
      iii. 40% U.S. Treasury Bonds
      iv. 10% Growth and Income Funds
      v. 10% Growth Funds
   b. Risk Level II: ___Conservative___ Growth & Income
      i. 5% Money Market Funds
      ii. 20% U.S. Treasury Bonds
      iii. 40% Income Funds
      iv. 25% Growth and Income Funds
      v. 10% Growth Funds

c. Risk Level III: __Aggressive__ Growth
   i. 10% Money Market Funds
   ii. 30% Growth and Income Funds
   iii. 30% Aggressive Growth Funds
   iv. 30% Income Funds

Lesson 18: Investing for Your Future

STUDENT RESPONSE
IMPROVEMENT ACTION PLAN

What I need to change:_____

What? I define my goal as this achievable result. What will be my final outcome?

My Answer:_____

_____

Why? This is why I need to accomplish my goal.

My Answer:_____

_____

Who? Who will be involved in making me successful?

My Answer:_____

_____

Where? Where will I get started? In what area will I begin?

My Answer:_____

_____

How? How will I accomplish what I want to achieve? How will I measure my progress?

My Answer:_____

_____

When? When will I begin working on achieving this goal?

My Answer:_____

_____

Lesson Nineteen

Planning for Retirement

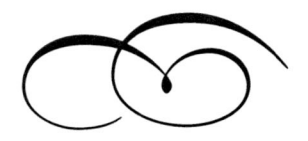

Then the LORD answered me and said:
"Write the vision and make it plain on tablets,
that he may run who reads it."
HABAKKUK 2:2 (NKJV)

Age-based retirement arbitrarily severs productive persons from their livelihood,
squanders their talents, scars their health, strains an already overburdened
Social Security system, and drives many elderly people into poverty and despair.
Ageism is as odious as racism and sexism.
NORMAN VINCENT PEALE

Preparation for old age should begin not later than one's teens.
A life which is empty of purpose until 65
will not suddenly become filled on retirement.
DWIGHT L. MOODY

Lesson Nineteen

Planning for Retirement

1. **Home Ownership**
   a. Home ownership is the first step toward a secure __retirement__ future.
   b. Buying a home is more expensive than the first-time homebuyer can imagine.
   c. The greatest difficulty is __accumulating__ the necessary sum to cover the down payment and closing costs.
   d. Some lenders require a 10-20% down payment and closing costs can be 5% or more of the total purchase price, but are usually between 1-4%.
   e. Regularly saving and __investing__ those savings make owning your own home possible.

There is no secret to saving. It is just a matter of living beneath your means.

---

2. **Saving for the First House**
   a. The short-term __sacrifice__ of foregoing pleasant, but unnecessary, luxuries is worth the long-term benefits of owning a home.
   b. When you get paid, set aside savings first.
   c. Conservatively invest your __savings__ so it will earn you money.
   d. US government securities, CDs, zero coupon treasury bonds and low-risk mutual equity funds should be considered.
   e. Mutual funds are recommendable.
   f. Real estate is a __solid__ investment because, while your home increases in value, your mortgage payment does not.

Biblical Principles for Financial Success Teacher Workbook

    g. Home ownership involves certain tax advantages.

    h. By the time you want to retire, you can ___enjoy___ your home at low or no cost or sell and buy a smaller home at no cost.

    i. Rent payments only increase, never decrease.

3. **Strategies for Retirement Planning**
    a. Know your ___retirement___ needs.
    b. Know your future financial needs.
    c. Know your housing needs.
    d. Know your ___health___ needs.
    e. Learn about your employer's pension or profit-sharing plan.
    f. Contribute to a tax-sheltered savings plan.
    g. Find out about your social security benefits.
    h. Put money into an IRA – individual retirement account.
    i. Protect your savings.
    j. Follow basic investment principles.
    k. Remember the rule of 72.

    To discover when your ___investment___ will double, divide 72 by the annual compound interest rate you expect to earn. If the rate is 7.2%, it will take 10 years to double your money.

    l. Ask questions.

4. **Vehicles for Growing Your Retirement Savings**
    a. Buy a home, contribute to an IRA and a deferred income plan such as a 401(k).
    b. Do your own ___research___ because CPAs, financial planners and bankers are trying to sell you something.

5. **Never Too Early, Never Too Late**
    a. Start saving for retirement as soon as possible.
    b. The power of compound interest takes a little bit early on and makes it worth more than a lot invested later in life.

c. Save ___small___ amounts on a weekly or monthly basis and it will turn into a lot bigger amount.

d. It's never too late to start saving and if you start later in life, put away as much as you possibly can.

6. **Failing to Plan**
   a. Be ___prepared___ for inflation, a sometimes down economy and the possibility of corporate fraud.
   b. Conserve not just principal, but purchasing power – the difference between earned interest and what inflation will take away.

7. **Living on Less or Living on More**
   a. It is a ___misconception___ that life will be cheaper when you are retired.
   b. In addition to higher medical, food, fuel, clothing, transportation and insurance costs, taxes will likely increase.

> **No one actively plans to fail in providing for a comfortable old age. They simply fail to plan.**

8. **Social Security Benefits**
   a. Social security will likely not be able to ___provide___ very much security for those now 40 or younger.
   b. Family sizes also do not always decrease upon retirement.
   c. Prepare your ___children___ as best you can to live independently.

9. **Living for the Moment**
   Live for the moment with 90% of your disposable income and save 10% for retirement.

10. **How Much Do I Need?**
    a. Most financial planners feel that you need 60-90% of the _income_ earned at the time of retirement.
    b. Consider planning for extra expenses such as travel and medical.

11. **The Inflation Concern**
    a. If you earn 7% on your _investments_, remember that 4% inflation reduces your purchasing power to 3%.
    b. Your after-tax return on savings and investments should exceed inflation.
    c. Divide the current inflation rate by 100 less your tax bracket. The percentage earned on your investment must exceed this number for your retirement savings to grow.
    d. Social security can be drawn upon at 62, but the _benefit_ is reduced. The longer you wait, the more beneficial.

12. **How Will My Retirement Be Funded?**
    a. Request an _estimate_ of your expected annual pension from your employee benefits department.
    b. Frequent job changes can seriously impact retirement benefits.

13. **Retirement Investment Products**
    a. Tax-Advantaged Retirement Products
    b. Employer-Sponsored Retirement Plans
    c. Cash Equivalents / Money Markets
    d. Income Investments
    e. Growth and _Income_ Investments
    f. Growth Investments
    g. Annuities
    h. Mutual Funds

Lesson 19: Planning for Retirement

STUDENT RESPONSE
IMPROVEMENT ACTION PLAN

What I need to change:_____

What? I define my goal as this achievable result. What will be my final outcome?

My Answer:_____

_____

Why? This is why I need to accomplish my goal.

My Answer:_____

_____

Who? Who will be involved in making me successful?

My Answer:_____

_____

Where? Where will I get started? In what area will I begin?

My Answer:_____

_____

How? How will I accomplish what I want to achieve? How will I measure my progress?

My Answer:_____

_____

When? When will I begin working on achieving this goal?

My Answer:_____

_____

Lesson Twenty

Preparing for the Unexpected

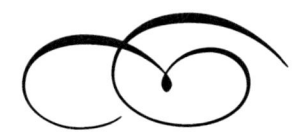

Go and make further preparation. . . .
I Samuel 23:22

Spectacular achievement is always preceded
by spectacular preparation.
Robert H. Schuller

Lesson Twenty

Preparing for the Unexpected

1. **Natural Disasters**
   a. Inventory your belongings.
   b. Use a ___video___ tape.
   c. Record make, model and serial numbers.

2. **Loss of Employment**
   The possibility of losing one's job should be ___incentive___ enough to live free of debt.

3. **Saving for Emergencies**
   a. Three to six months' living expenses should be kept in safe, liquid cash investments for emergencies.
   b. Some ___emergencies___ to save for:
      i. Travel expenses to family or relatives in case of illness or death
      ii. Deductibles or co-payments on ___medical___ expenses
      iii. Auto insurance deductibles and temporary auto replacement, in case of an accident
      iv. Auto repairs
      v. Travel and gift expenses for ___weddings___ of family and friends
      vi. Replacement of appliances that could break down
   c. Plan for these emergencies when you make your budget each year.

d. Keep your emergency fund in…
   i. A savings account
   ii. Bank money market deposit accounts
   iii. Certificates of deposit (CDs)
   iv. Money market funds

4. **Automatic Savings**
   a. If you are starting with no emergency fund, budget to pay __monthly__ toward this.
   b. Have it automatically deducted from your paycheck and put in a money market fund.
   c. Whenever you get a __raise__, increase your savings by that amount.

5. **Keeping Track of Important Papers**
   a. Your will
   b. Your personal papers
   c. Your advisors
   d. Your debts
   e. Your insurance
   f. Your savings and __investment__ records
   g. Your safe-deposit box

6. **Reviewing Your Insurance**
   a. Renters and homeowners insurance
   b. Umbrella insurance
   c. Disability insurance
   d. Life insurance
   e. Auto insurance

7. **Proactively Prepared**
   While no one can __foresee__ every situation; it is good to prepare responsibly as outlined above, and then to trust God.

Lesson 20: Preparing for the Unexpected

STUDENT RESPONSE
IMPROVEMENT ACTION PLAN

What I need to change:_____

What? I define my goal as this achievable result. What will be my final outcome?

My Answer:_____

_____

Why? This is why I need to accomplish my goal.

My Answer:_____

_____

Who? Who will be involved in making me successful?

My Answer:_____

_____

Where? Where will I get started? In what area will I begin?

My Answer:_____

_____

How? How will I accomplish what I want to achieve? How will I measure my progress?

My Answer:_____

_____

When? When will I begin working on achieving this goal?

My Answer:_____

_____

Answer Key

Lesson 1

1.a	principles
2.	anticipate
3.a.	guiding
3.c.	provider
4.a.	contentment
4.c.	opportunity
5.a.	harm
5.c.	human
6.b.	morals
7.a.	rob
7.c.	honor
8.a.	profit
8.c.	clean
9.a.	pre-occupied
9.c.	tool
9.e.	eternally
10.b.	action
11.	economy
12.a.	little
13.a.	possessing
13.b.	riches
14.a.	goods
14.b.	invest
15.a.	God
15.c.	Desire
16.a.	owner
16.c.	eternal

Lesson 2

1.b.	water
2.a.	increase
2.c.	enriches
3.a.	obligation
3.c.	wealth
4.a.	plant
4.c.	always
4.e.	reap
4.g.	harvest
5.a.	owns
5.b.	Money
5.b.ii)	accountability
5.b.iv)	exposed
5.b.vi)	blessing
5.b.viii)	actions
5.c.ii)	further
5.c.iii)	everything
5.d.ii)	priorities
5.d.iv)	trigger

Lesson 3

1.	give
3.	nothing
4.	ability
5.	belong
6.	source
7.	abundant
8.	important
9.a.	stewards
9.c.	tithed
9.e.	tithe
11.	tithed
14.	seed
16.	generosity

Lesson 4

1.	cheerfully
3.	(Bullets)
	owns
	proactive
	plenty
	advanced
	temporary
	systematic
	learning
	sacrificial
	faithfulness
	working
	refreshing
	understanding
	contentment
	hope
	guarding
	blessing
	financial
	full
	trusting
	right
	providing
	diligence
	enjoying
	freedom

Answer Key

Lesson 5

1.a.	scriptural
1.b.	possessions
3.	overseeing
4.	responsibility
6.	complete
7.	entire
9.	everything
11.	obey
13.	manage
19.	exercise
23.	disciplined
25.a.	laziness
25.c.	gift

Lesson 6

1.a.	wisely
1.c.	investing
2.a.	invest
3.	important
4.	purpose
5.	account
6.c.	regular
7.	control
9.	communicate
10.a.i)	participation
10.b.i)	share
10.c.	Ready
11.a.	Mean
11.d.	Thinks
11.f.	Said
12.b.	objective
13.b.	main
14.a.	evaluation
14.c.	attention
15.a.	uncomfortable
16.a.	common
17.b.	positive
18.	contract
19.a.	reception
20.a.	negative
21.	communication

Lesson 7

1.a.	understand
1.d.	expenditures
2.	judgement
3.b.	choice
3.c.	attitude
3.d.i.	fulfillment
4.a.	alternative
4.c.ii.	managing
4.c.iii.	decision
5.a.	outcome
5.c.	careful
6.a.	mistakes
6.c.	experience
6.e.	Review

Lesson 8

1.	satisfaction
2.	recognizing
4.	define
6.	evaluate

Lesson 9

1.	objectives
5.	diligent
6.	constantly
7.b.	target
7.d.	timeline
9.	potential
10b.	determination
16.c.	Structure
16.f.	Habit
17.b.	Financial
18.b.	right
18.e.	build
18.h.	prepares
19.c.	standards
19.e.	detailed
21.a.	planning
21.b.	developing
22.b.	Ideas
23.g.	Work
24.a.	measurements
25.e.	Updating

Lesson 10

1.a.	account
1.c.	discipline
2.a.	expenses
2.b.i.	picture
2.b.iii.	fixed
2.b.v.	daily
2.d.i.	categories
2.d.iii.	discretionary
2.g.i.	spending
2.g.ii.	mathematical
2.g.iv.	framework

Lesson 11

1.a.	free
1.c.	enhance
2.	(Bullets)
	tool
	opens
	keep
	team
	balance
	expenses
	goals
	realistically
	temptations
	gives
	advantage

Lesson 12

1.b.	control
2.c.	analyze
3.	worksheet
4.b.	save
4.f.	impulse
4.k.	interest-bearing
4.o.	balance
4.r.	budget
5.a.	promptly
5.d.	two
5.g.	record
5.i.	remember
6.c.	Budget
6.g.	Debt
6.l.	Thinking

Lesson 13

1.b.	long-range
1.f.	increases
2.c.	stumbling
3.b.	Mutual
4.c.	credit
4.h.	retirement
4.l.	spending
4.n.i.	afford
4.o.	doing
4.o.iv.	lunch
4.o.vii.	appreciate
4.o.xi.	recreation
4.o.xiii.	free
4.p.	personal
4.r.	Compound

Lesson 14

1.	reveal
1.a.	debt
1.c.	Right
1.d.	Self-controlled
1.e.	Problem
1.f.	Bondage
1.h.	Borrowing
1.l.	Impending
1.o.	Credit
1.r.	extension
1.w.	Spotless
2.e.	information
3.a.	accounts
3.e.	delinquent
3.h.	fraudulent

4.f.	Range
5.b.	balances
8.a.	Rebuild
8.d.	mistakes
9.a.ii	consolidate

Lesson 15

1.	expenses
3.	essential
4.	habits
6.	heroism
8.	small
9.	balance
10.a.	owe
10.d.	plan
12.	prioritizing
13.	impressed
15.a.	net
15.d.	monthly
15.g.	payoff
15.m.	current
18.	families
19.	communicate
20.	totally
22.d.	confidently
22.i.	anticipate
22.k.	specific
25.	repay
26.	reward

Lesson 16

3.b.	spend
3.d.	receive

Answer Key

5. (bullets)
- advice
- cosigning
- questionable
- unnecessary
- afford
- spending
- expensive
- savings
- high-risk
- water
- alternatives
- medical
- yourself
- buying
- deductibles
- spending
- better
- emergency
- necessary
- plans
- borrow
- grocery
- utility
- professional
- incurring
- checkbook
- coupons
- ten
- six

Lesson 17

1.a. borrowing
1. ensure

2.b. personal
2.e. "fraud"
3.d. Good

Lesson 18

2.b. Time
3.d. Diversify
3.f. Foolishness
3.g. Highest
3.j. Accurate
3.m. Small
4.a. stick
4.d. regular
5.a. Low-cost
5.c. Well-balanced
7.c. Treasury
7.h. Municipal
7.k.ii. Securities
7.l. Stock
8.a. Preservation
8.b. Conservative
8.c. Aggressive

Lesson 19

1.a. retirement
1.c. accumulating
1.e. investing
2.a. sacrifice
2.c. savings
2.f. solid
2.h. enjoy

3.a. retirement
3.d. health
3.k. investment
4.b. research
5.c. small
6.a. prepared
7.a. misconception
8.a. provide
8.c. children
10.a. income
11.a. investments
11.d. benefit
12.a. estimate
13.e. Income

Lesson 20

1.b. video
2. incentive
3.b. Emergencies
3.b.ii. medical
3.b.v. weddings
4.a. monthly
4.c. raise
5.f. Investment
7. foresee

Source Material

21 Unbreakable Laws of Success, Max Anders, Thomas Nelson, 1996
A Christian Guide to Prosperity; Fries & Taylor, California: Communications Research, 1984
A Look At Stewardship, Word Aflame Publications, 2001
American Savings Education Council (http://www.asec.org)
Anointed For Business, Ed Silvoso, Regal, 2002
Avoiding Common Financial Mistakes, Ron Blue, Navpress, 1991
Baker Encyclopedia of the Bible; Walter Elwell, Michigan: Baker Book House, 1988
Becoming The Best, Barry Popplewell, England: Gower Publishing Company Limited, 1988
Business Proverbs, Steve Marr, Fleming H. Revell, 2001
Cheapskate Monthly, Mary Hunt
Commentary on the Old Testament; Keil Delitzsch, Michigan: Eerdmans Publishing, 1986
Crown Financial Ministries, various publications
Customers As Partners, Chip Bell, Texas: Berrett Koehler Publishers, 1994
Cut Your Bills in Half; Pennsylvania: Rodale Press, Inc., 1989
Debt-Free Living, Larry Burkett, Dimensions, 2001
Die Broke, Stephen M. Pollan & Mark Levine, HarperBusiness, 1997
Double Your Profits, Bob Fifer, Virginia: Lincoln Hall Press, 1993
Eerdmans' Handbook to the Bible, Michigan: William B. Eerdmans Publishing Company, 1987
Eight Steps to Seven Figures, Charles B. Carlson, Double Day, 2000
Everyday Life in Bible Times; Washington DC: National Geographic Society, 1967
Financial Dominion, Norvel Hayes, Harrison House, 1986
Financial Freedom, Larry Burkett, Moody Press, 1991
Financial Freedom, Patrick Clements, VMI Publishers, 2003
Financial Peace, Dave Ramsey, Viking Press, 2003
Financial Self-Defense; Charles Givens, New York: Simon And Schuster, 1990
Flood Stage, Oral Roberts, 1981
Generous Living, Ron Blue, Zondervan, 1997
Get It All Done, Tony and Robbie Fanning, New York:Pennsylvania: Chilton Book, 1979
Getting Out of Debt, Howard Dayton, Tyndale House, 1986
Getting Out of Debt, Mary Stephenson, Fact Sheet 436, University of Maryland Cooperative Extension Service, 1988
Giving and Tithing, Larry Burkett, Moody Press, 1991
God's Plan For Giving, John MacArthur, Jr., Moody Press, 1985
God's Will is Prosperity, Gloria Copeland, Harrison House, 1978

Source Material

Great People of the Bible and How They Lived; New York: Reader's Digest, 1974
How Others Can Help You Get Out of Debt; Esther M. Maddux, Circular 759-3,
How To Make A Business Plan That Works, Henderson, North Island Sound Limited, 1989
How To Manage Your Money, Larry Burkett, Moody Press, 1999
How to Personally Profit From the Laws of Success, Sterling Sill, NIFP, Inc., 1978
How to Plan for Your Retirement; New York: Corrigan & Kaufman, Longmeadow Press, 1985
Is God Your Source?, Oral Roberts, 1992
It's Not Luck, Eliyahu Goldratt, Great Barrington, MA: The North River Press, 1994
Jesus CEO, Laurie Beth Jones, Hyperion, 1995
John Avanzini Answers Your Questions About Biblical Economics, Harrison House, 1992
Living on Less and Liking It More, Maxine Hancock, Chicago, Illinois: Moody Press, 1976
Making It Happen; Charles Conn, New Jersey: Fleming H. Revell Company, 1981
Master Your Money Or It Will Master You, Arlo E. Moehlenpah, Doing Good Ministries, 1999
Master Your Money; Ron Blue, Tennessee: Thomas Nelson, Inc. 1986
Miracle of Seed Faith, Oral Roberts, 1970
Mississippi State University Extension Service
Money, Possessions, and Eternity, Randy Alcorn, Tyndale House, 2003
More Than Enough, David Ramsey, Penguin Putnam Inc, 2002
Moving the Hand of God, John Avanzini, Harrison House, 1990
Multiplication, Tommy Barnett, Creation House, 1997
NebFacts, Nebraska Cooperative Extension
New York Post
One Up On Wall Street; New York: Peter Lynch, Simon And Schuster, 1989
Personal Finances, Larry Burkett, Moody Press, 1991
Portable MBA in Finance and Accounting; Livingstone, Canada: John Wiley & Sons, Inc., 1992
Principle Centered Leadership, Stephen R. Covey, New York: Summit Books, 1991
Principles of Financial Management, Kolb & DeMong, Texas: Business Publications, Inc., 1988
Rapid Debt Reduction Strategies, John Avanzini, HIS Publishing, 1990
Real Wealth, Wade Cook, Arizona: Regency Books, 1985
See You At The Top, Zig Ziglar, Louisianna: Pelican Publishing Company, 1977
Seed Faith Commentary on the Holy Bible, Oral Roberts, Pinoak Publications, 1975
Sharkproof, Harvey Mackay, New York: HarperCollins Publishers, 1993
Smart Money, Ken and Daria Dolan, New York: Random House, Inc., 1988
Strong's Concordance, Tennessee: Crusade Bible Publishers, Inc.,
Success by Design, Peter Hirsch, Bethany House, 2002
Success is the Quality of your Journey, Jennifer James, New York: Newmarket Press, 1983
Swim with the Sharks Without Being Eaten Alive, Harvey Mackay, William Morrow, 1988

Biblical Principles for Financial Success   Teacher Workbook

The Almighty and the Dollar; Jim McKeever, Oregon: Omega Publications, 1981
The Challenge, Robert Allen, New York: Simon And Schuster, 1987
The Family Financial Workbook, Larry Burkett, Moody Press, 2002
The Management Methods of Jesus, Bob Briner, Thomas Nelson, 1996
The Millionaire Next Door, Thomas Stanley & William Danko, Pocket Books, 1996
The Money Book for Kids, Nancy Burgeson, Troll Associates,1992
The Money Book for King's Kids; Harold E. Hill, New Jersey: Fleming H. Revell Company, 1984
The Seven Habits of Highly Effective People, Stephen Covey, New York: Simon And Schuster, 1989
The Wealthy Barber, David Chilton, California: Prima Publishing, 1991
Theological Wordbook of the Old Testament, Chicago, Illinois: Moody Press, 1981
Treasury of Courage and Confidence, Norman Vincent Peale, New York: Doubleday & Co., 1970
True Prosperity, Dick Iverson, Bible Temple Publishing, 1993
Trust God For Your Finances, Jack Hartman, Lamplight Publications, 1983
University of Georgia Cooperative Extension Service, 1985
Virginia Cooperative Extension
Webster's Unabridged Dictionary, Dorset & Baber, 1983
What Is an Entrepreneur; David Robinson, MA: Kogan Page Limited, 1990
Word Meanings in the New Testament, Ralph Earle, Michigan: Baker Book House, 1986
Word Pictures in the New Testament; Robertson, Michigan: Baker Book House, 1930
Word Studies in the New Testament; Vincent, New York: Charles Scribner's Sons, 1914
Worth
You Can Be Financially Free, George Fooshee, Jr., 1976, Fleming H. Revell Company.
Your Key to God's Bank, Rex Humbard, 1977
Your Money Counts, Howard, Dayton, Tyndale House, 1997
Your Money Management, MaryAnn Paynter, Circular 1271, University of Illinois Cooperative Extension Service, 1987.
Your Money Matters, Malcolm MacGregor, Bethany Fellowship, Inc., 1977
Your Road to Recovery, Oral Roberts, Oliver Nelson, 1986

Comments On Sources

Over the years I have collected bits and pieces of interesting material, written notes on sermons I've heard, jotted down comments on financial articles I've read, and gathered a lot of great information. It is unfortunate that I didn't record the sources of all of these notes in my earlier years. I gratefully extend my appreciation to the many writers, authors, teachers and pastors from whose articles and sermons I have gleaned much insight.

Rich Brott

ONLINE RESOURCES

American Savings Education Council (http://www.asec.org)
Bloomberg.com (http://www.bloomberg.com)
Bureau of the Public Debt Online (http://www.publicdebt.treas.gov)
BusinessWeek (http://www.businessweek.com)
Charles Schwab & Co., Inc. (http://www.schwab.com)
Consumer Federation of America (http://www.consumerfed.org)
Debt Advice.org (http://www.debtadvice.org)
Federal Reserve System (http://www.federalreserve.gov)
Fidelity Investments (http://www.fidelity.com)
Financial Planning Association (http://www.fpanet.org)
Forbes (www.forbes.com)
Fortune Magazine (http://www.fortune.com)
Generous Giving (http://www.generousgiving.org/)
Investing for Your Future (http://www.investing.rutgers.edu)
Kiplinger Magazine (http://www.kiplinger.com/)
Money Magazine (http://money.cnn.com)
MorningStar (http://www.morningstar.com)
MSN Money (http://moneycentral.msn.com)
Muriel Siebert (http://www.siebertnet.com)
National Center on Education and the Economy (http://www.ncee.org)
National Foundation for Credit Counseling (http://www.nfcc.org)
Quicken (http://www.quicken.com)
Smart Money (http://www.smartmoney.com)
Social Security Online (http://www.ssa.gov)
Standard & Poor's (http://www2.standardandpoors.com)
The Dollar Stretcher, Gary Foreman, (http://www.stretcher.com)
The Vanguard Group (http://flagship.vanguard.com)
U.S. Securities and Exchange Commission (http://www.sec.gov)
Yahoo! Finance (http://finance.yahoo.com)

Source Material

Magazine Resources

Business Week
Consumer Reports
Forbes
Kiplinger's Personal Finance
Money
Smart Money
US News and World Report

Biblical Principles for Financial Success   Teacher Workbook

NEWSPAPER RESOURCES

Barrons
Investors Business Daily
USA Today
Wall Street Journal
Washington Times

Additional Resources by Rich Brott

5 Simple Keys to Financial Freedom

Change Your Life Forever!

By Rich Brott

6" x 9", 108 pages
ISBN 1-60185-022-0
ISBN (EAN) 978-1-60185-022-5

abc Book Publishing

Order online at:
www.amazon.com
www.barnesandnoble.com
www.booksamillion.com
www.citychristianpublishing.com
www.walmart.com

www.AbcBookPublishing.com

Additional Resources by Rich Brott

**10 Life-Changing Attitudes
That Will Make You
a Financial Success**

By Rich Brott

6" x 9", 108 pages
ISBN 1-60185-021-2
ISBN (EAN) 978-1-60185-021-8

abc Book Publishing

Order online at:
www.amazon.com
www.barnesandnoble.com
www.booksamillion.com
www.citychristianpublishing.com
www.walmart.com

www.AbcBookPublishing.com

Additional Resources by Rich Brott

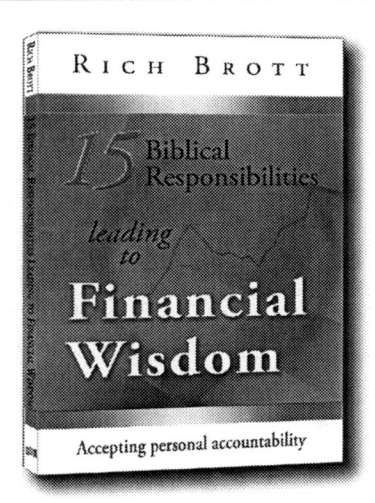

15 Biblical Responsibilities Leading to Financial Wisdom

Accepting Personal Accountability

By Rich Brott

6" x 9", 120 pages
ISBN 1-60185-010-7
ISBN (EAN) 978-1-60185-010-2

abc Book Publishing

Order online at:
www.amazon.com
www.barnesandnoble.com
www.booksamillion.com
www.citychristianpublishing.com
www.walmart.com

www.AbcBookPublishing.com

Additional Resources by Rich Brott

30 Biblical Principles for Managing Your Money

Insights that Will Set You Free!

By Rich Brott

6" x 9", 160 pages
ISBN 1-60185-012-3
ISBN (EAN) 978-1-60185-012-6

Book Publishing

Order online at:
www.amazon.com
www.barnesandnoble.com
www.booksamillion.com
www.citychristianpublishing.com
www.walmart.com

www.AbcBookPublishing.com

Additional Resources by Rich Brott

35 Keys to Financial Independence

Finding the Freedom You Seek!

By Rich Brott

6" x 9", 176 pages
ISBN 1-60185-020-4
ISBN (EAN) 978-1-60185-020-1

Book Publishing

Order online at:
www.amazon.com
www.barnesandnoble.com
www.booksamillion.com
www.citychristianpublishing.com
www.walmart.com

www.AbcBookPublishing.com

Additional Resources by Rich Brott

A Biblical Perspective on Tithing & Giving

A Believer's Stewardship Guide

By Rich Brott

6" x 9", 172 pages
ISBN 1-60185-000-X
ISBN (EAN) 978-1-60185-000-3

abc Book Publishing

Order online at:
www.amazon.com
www.barnesandnoble.com
www.booksamillion.com
www.citychristianpublishing.com
www.walmart.com

www.AbcBookPublishing.com

Additional Resources by Rich Brott

Basic Principles for Maximizing Your Personal Cash Flow

7 Steps to Financial Freedom!

By Rich Brott

6" x 9", 120 pages
ISBN 1-60185-019-0
ISBN (EAN) 978-1-60185-019-5

abc Book Publishing

Order online at:
www.amazon.com
www.barnesandnoble.com
www.booksamillion.com
www.citychristianpublishing.com
www.walmart.com

www.AbcBookPublishing.com

Additional Resources by Rich Brott

Basic Principles of Conservative Investing

9 Principles You Must Follow

By Rich Brott

6" x 9", 116 pages
ISBN 1-60185-018-2
ISBN (EAN) 978-1-60185-018-8

abc Book Publishing

Order online at:
www.amazon.com
www.barnesandnoble.com
www.booksamillion.com
www.citychristianpublishing.com
www.walmart.com

www.AbcBookPublishing.com

Additional Resources by Rich Brott

Biblical Principles for Staying Out of Debt

7 Things You Must Know!

By Rich Brott

6" x 9", 120 pages
ISBN 1-60185-009-3
ISBN (EAN) 978-1-60185-009-6

abc Book Publishing

Order online at:
www.amazon.com
www.barnesandnoble.com
www.booksamillion.com
www.citychristianpublishing.com
www.walmart.com

www.AbcBookPublishing.com

Additional Resources by Rich Brott

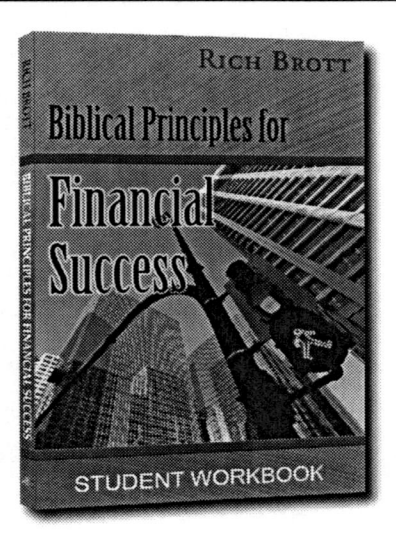

Biblical Principles for Financial Success

Student Workbook

By Rich Brott

7.5" x 9.25", 228 pages
ISBN 1-60185-016-6
ISBN (EAN) 978-1-60185-016-4

abc Book Publishing

Order online at:
www.amazon.com
www.barnesandnoble.com
www.booksamillion.com
www.citychristianpublishing.com
www.walmart.com

www.AbcBookPublishing.com

Additional Resources by Rich Brott

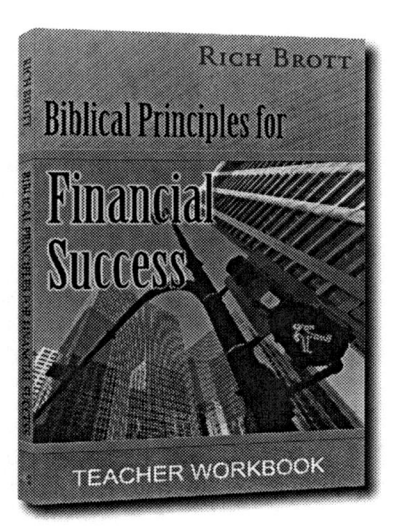

Biblical Principles for Financial Success

Teacher Workbook

By Rich Brott

7.5" x 9.25", 228 pages
ISBN 1-60185-015-8
ISBN (EAN) 978-1-60185-015-7

Book Publishing

Order online at:
www.amazon.com
www.barnesandnoble.com
www.booksamillion.com
www.citychristianpublishing.com
www.walmart.com

www.AbcBookPublishing.com

Additional Resources by Rich Brott

Biblical Principles that Create Success through Productivity

How God Blesses Our Work Ethic

By Rich Brott

6" x 9", 224 pages
ISBN 1-60185-007-7
ISBN (EAN) 978-1-60185-007-2

Book Publishing

Order online at:
www.amazon.com
www.barnesandnoble.com
www.booksamillion.com
www.citychristianpublishing.com
www.walmart.com

www.AbcBookPublishing.com

Additional Resources by Rich Brott

Business, Occupations, Professions & Vocations in the Bible

By Rich Brott

6" x 9", 212 pages
ISBN 1-60185-014-X
ISBN (EAN) 978-1-60185-014-0

abc Book Publishing

Order online at:
www.amazon.com
www.barnesandnoble.com
www.booksamillion.com
www.citychristianpublishing.com
www.walmart.com

www.AbcBookPublishing.com

Additional Resources by Rich Brott

Biblical Principles for Success in Personal Finance

Your Roadmap to Financial Independence

By Rich Brott

7.5" x 10", 519 pages
ISBN 0-914936-72-7
ISBN (EAN) 978-0-914936-72-5

abc Book Publishing

Order online at:
www.amazon.com
www.barnesandnoble.com
www.booksamillion.com
www.citychristianpublishing.com
www.walmart.com

www.AbcBookPublishing.com

Additional Resources by Rich Brott

Biblical Principles for Building a Successful Business

A Practical Guide to Assessing, Evaluating, and Growing a Successful Cutting-Edge Enterprise in Today's Business Environment

By Rich Brott & Frank Damazio

7.5" x 10", 477 pages
ISBN 1-59383-027-0
ISBN (EAN) 978-1-59383-027-4

abc Book Publishing

Order online at:
www.amazon.com
www.barnesandnoble.com
www.booksamillion.com
www.citychristianpublishing.com
www.walmart.com

www.AbcBookPublishing.com

Additional Resources by Rich Brott

Biblical Principles for Becoming Debt Free!

*Rescue Your Life and
Liberate Your Future!*

By Rich Brott & Frank Damazio

7.5" x 10", 320 pages
ISBN 1-886849-85-4
ISBN 978-1-886849-85-3

abc Book Publishing

Order online at:
www.amazon.com
www.barnesandnoble.com
www.booksamillion.com
www.citychristianpublishing.com
www.walmart.com

www.AbcBookPublishing.com

Additional Resources by Rich Brott

Biblical Principles for Releasing Financial Provision!

Obtaining the Favor of God in Your Personal and Business World

By Rich Brott

7.5" x 10", 456 pages
ISBN 1-59383-021-1
ISBN (EAN) 978-1-59383-021-2

abc Book Publishing

Order online at:
www.amazon.com
www.barnesandnoble.com
www.booksamillion.com
www.citychristianpublishing.com
www.walmart.com

www.AbcBookPublishing.com

Additional Resources by Rich Brott

Family Finance Handbook

Discovering the Blessing of Financial Freedom

By Rich Brott & Frank Damazio

7.5" x 10", 288 pages
ISBN 1-914936-60-3
ISBN 978-1-914936-60-2

abc Book Publishing

Order online at:
www.amazon.com
www.barnesandnoble.com
www.booksamillion.com
www.citychristianpublishing.com
www.walmart.com

www.AbcBookPublishing.com

Printed in the United States
107902LV00003B/23-32/A